The Defensive Value Investor

The Defensive Value Investor

A complete step-by-step guide to building a high-yield, low-risk share portfolio

By John Kingham

HARRIMAN HOUSE LTD

18 College Street

Petersfield

Hampshire

GU31 4AD

GREAT BRITAIN

Tel: +44 (0)1730 233870

Email: enquiries@harriman-house.com

Website: www.harriman-house.com

First published in Great Britain in 2016

Copyright © John Kingham

The right of John Kingham to be identified as the author has been asserted in accordance with the Copyright, Design and Patents Act 1988.

Print ISBN: 978-0-85719-398-8

eBook ISBN: 978-0-85719-533-3

British Library Cataloguing in Publication Data

A CIP catalogue record for this book can be obtained from the British Library.

About the Author

John Kingham is an experienced private investor, investment blogger and newsletter publisher. His professional background is in computer software for the insurance industry, where he worked for clients ranging from Lloyd's syndicates to some of the world's largest general insurers.

In 2011 John left the computer software industry and began publishing *UK Value Investor*, a monthly newsletter for defensive value investors.

John currently lives in Kent with his wife and son. His website can be found at: www.ukvalueinvestor.com

Every owner of a physical copy of this version of

The Defensive Value Investor

can download the eBook for free direct from us at Harriman House, in a format that can be read on any eReader, tablet or smartphone.

Simply head to:

ebooks.harriman-house.com/defensivevalue

to get your free eBook now.

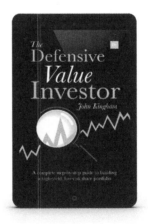

Preface

What this book covers

This book takes you step-by-step through a simple but comprehensive strategy for investing in the stock market. The strategy is called defensive value investing for obvious reasons: it combines elements of both defensive investing and value investing.

On the one hand, defensive investing is about buying the shares of high-quality companies that have been around for many years, paying and steadily growing their dividends. It also goes beyond stock selection and requires some thought about how a portfolio is structured, such as how many companies it should hold, which industries and countries those companies operate in, and so on.

On the other hand, value investing focuses primarily on whether or not a company's shares represent good value for money at their current price. A value investor would say that even if you found the most defensive company in the world, it might still turn out to be a bad investment if you pay too much for it.

Defensive value investing is therefore about buying relatively defensive companies at value for money prices. The specific strategy in this book is based on a series of rules of thumb which turn the theory into a checklist of simple and actionable statements.

I'll cover enough theory so that you can clearly understand why each part of the strategy is there, but this is primarily a practical book to be used as an aid to real-world investing, rather than just as an interesting read.

To help you see how this strategy can be applied in the real world, I've included many examples of actual investments I have made in recent years.

Who this book is for

This book is for you if you're looking to invest directly in the shares of individual companies rather than, or in addition to, collective investment vehicles such as unit trusts. More specifically, it is for those who want to invest in relatively large and successful companies, usually with high dividend yields and long records of profitable dividend growth.

You should be looking to invest at least £30,000 into a broadly diversified portfolio of defensive value stocks. I think that amount is a reasonable minimum because the strategy involves holding around 30 stocks, which gives an average investment per holding of £1000. At that size a typical £10 broker fee on both the buy and sell trade would amount to 2% of each investment, which is the most I would want to pay. With smaller portfolios these fixed broker fees can become a significant drag on returns.

Defensive value investing is a long-term investment approach suitable for long-term investors. Although *long term* is somewhat ambiguous, I would typically expect each stock to be held for between one and ten years, and around five years on average. This is not a get-rich-quick scheme.

The strategy requires at least one stock to be bought or sold each month, so this book is not really suitable for buy-and-hold or buy-and-forget investors. Having said that, any investment analysis should take no more than a few hours each month to carry out, so although this is an active investing strategy it is by no means full-time.

In terms of your existing knowledge, you should already have a basic understanding of investing and company accounts. You won't need to be an accountant, but you should at least know what balance sheets, income statements and cash flow statements are. You should also understand basic terms such as: assets and liabilities; revenues, expenses and profits; and market capitalisation, dividends and rights issues.

I have tried to explain everything as clearly I can but if you find some of the terms or concepts unfamiliar I would suggest you read an introductory book first, such as Rodney Hobson's *Shares Made Simple*.

How this book is structured

This is very much a step-by-step book and each chapter builds upon the ideas laid down previously, so it's important that you read it in order. The chapters are divided into three parts and an appendix.

Part 1: Analysing a Company's Accounts

Most investors like to think about which company to buy next, so I'll cover that first. In this section, I'll go through how to select companies based on their past financial results, such as historic revenues, earnings and dividends. This is an important first step because a company's financial track record says a lot about how defensive that company might be.

What we'll be looking for here are companies with long and unbroken records of dividend payments, strong and consistent growth, good profitability and robust balance sheets.

We will also begin to look at whether or not a company's shares might be good value by comparing their current price against the historic earnings and dividends.

Part 2: Analysing a Company's Business

Having found a good company at an attractive price our next step is to build up a general understanding of what the company does and how it does it. After that we'll look at whether it has any durable competitive advantages and whether it might be a value trap (i.e. the company has some problems which mean it isn't worth as much as its past results would suggest).

The end of the company analysis process is marked by the final decision to buy or not to buy, where a degree of psychological commitment is reached before making any purchase. After all, long-term investors should hold their shares for a number of years and the last thing we want to do is sell them at the first sign of trouble.

Part 3: Managing Your Portfolio

Deciding which companies to buy is just one part of the investment puzzle. Once you've bought a company there are many other decisions to be made, such as what to do if the share price shoots up, what to do if the share price crashes, or what to do if a company announces bad news such as a dividend cut.

Looking beyond each individual holding, there are many other things which need to be considered at the portfolio level. These include how to make sure your portfolio is sufficiently diversified, how and when to make changes to your portfolio, and the importance of continued learning and improvement. I cover a wide range of these and similar topics in the third part of the book.

Appendix

The defensive value investing strategy requires ten years of financial data for each company that you analyse. Not all data providers carry ten years of data, so I have listed some of the ones I use in the appendix. I have also listed some of the other tools I use, such as software to track my portfolio's performance.

Although there is no complex maths in this book there are quite a few simple calculations, so I have included a link to my website where you can download some printable worksheets or spreadsheets, if you prefer. You can use these to analyse and compare companies and track the diversity of your portfolio.

Contents

About the Author   v
Preface   vii
Introduction   1

Part 1. Quantitative Analysis of Company Accounts   **7**
Chapter 1. Profitable Dividends   9
Chapter 2. Consistent Growth   19
Chapter 3. High Profitability   33
Chapter 4. Conservative Finances   50
Chapter 5. Low Valuation   85
Chapter 6. Defensiveness and Value Combined   101

Part 2. Qualitative Analysis of a Company's Business   **125**
Chapter 7. Value Traps   127
Chapter 8. Competitive Advantages   164
Chapter 9. Making a Final Decision   183

Part 3. Managing Your Portfolio   **187**
Chapter 10. Diversify Wisely   189
Chapter 11. Buy Slowly   203
Chapter 12. Hold Steadily   217
Chapter 13. Sell Deliberately   238
Chapter 14. Improve Continuously   257

Appendix   **273**

Rules of Thumb Checklist   **285**

Introduction

When I began investing in 1995 I took the sensible route and invested in a FTSE All-Share tracker fund. As a result my investments tracked the dot-com boom upwards during the late 1990s and then back down again in the early 2000s bear market. I saw the value of my portfolio double and then halve in just ten years, which was both exciting and terrifying in equal measure. I had almost no knowledge of the stock market and decided that I did not want to ride a rollercoaster I did not understand, so I sold everything and moved into the apparent safety of cash.

Like many other investors, I sold everything at the worst possible moment, in the depths of the 2003 bear market. It seemed like a good idea at the time but as a result I completely missed the market's rebound. As I sat there, metaphorically in the dust as the market sped away from me, I realised I had no idea what I was doing.

My response was to learn as much as I could about the stock market, economics, accounting and anything else that might make me a better investor. The problem is there are just so many theories, so many different approaches, that it's difficult to know which are sensible and which are barmy.

I tried out lots of different investment styles, but in the end it was the property market that turned me into a defensive value investor.

Back in 1996, shortly after I first invested in shares, I bought my first house. While the stock market went up and up and up, and then down and down and down, the property market only seemed to go up.

By 2000 my house had doubled in value and by 2004 it had doubled again. That just didn't make sense. The house and its surrounding area had not changed in the slightest. It wasn't an up and coming area, yet just eight years after I'd bought it, someone else was willing to pay four times as much for the same house.

I wanted to know if I could expect house prices to continue doubling every four years and, if not, why not.

What I discovered was that markets, whether for property or shares, could go through booms and busts, through periods of depression and euphoria. During these periods prices could go far higher or far lower than a calm and sensible buyer would be willing to pay. This was clearly true as I'd seen the stock market double in five years and halve in three, and I'd seen my house double in value twice over between 1996 and 2004.

The ability of UK-listed companies or my house to produce a cash income hadn't changed by anything like those amounts. The stock market was still made up of the same companies, producing more or less the same amount of profit and dividends in 2000 as they had in 1995, while my house was the same house, capable of producing only slightly more rent for a landlord in 2004 than it could have in 1997.

So it wasn't changes in the cash-generating abilities of companies or houses which had produced those large changes in their respective values, it was simply that people were willing to pay massively different prices for essentially the same assets at different points in time.

From that I learned a very important lesson, perhaps the most important lesson: the trick to boosting returns far beyond what you might normally expect given the economics of the underlying asset (whether a house or a company) was to buy when everybody else thought you were crazy to buy (like buying a house in 1996 when nobody was talking about property as an investment) and to sell when everybody else thought you were crazy to sell (like selling a house in 2004, when everybody wanted to be a property millionaire).

As the property market was already looking very expensive in 2004 on a price-to-earnings basis, and therefore unlikely to keep doubling every four years (and with hindsight, it didn't), I started reading up on how I could apply this sort of contrarian thinking to the stock market instead.

Eventually I found an old book called *The Intelligent Investor*, which was originally published in 1947. As you may know, it was written by a man called Benjamin Graham, who was Warren Buffett's mentor. That book became the bedrock upon which all of my investment efforts have since been based.

After a brief spell as a deep value investor – buying struggling but debt-free businesses for less than the scrap value of their assets – I re-read *The Intelligent Investor* and found exactly what I was looking for in a short list of rules for what Graham called defensive investors:

> "The selection of common stocks for the portfolio of the defensive investor is a relatively simple matter. Here we would suggest four rules to be followed:
>
> (1) There should be adequate though not excessive diversification. This might mean a minimum of ten different issues and a maximum of about thirty.
>
> (2) Each company selected should be large, prominent, and conservatively financed. Indefinite as these adjectives must be, their general sense is clear.
>
> (3) Each company should have a long record of continuous dividend payments.

(4) The price paid for each should be reasonable in relation to its average earnings for the last five years or longer. This would protect the investor against the common error of buying good stocks at high levels of the general market. It would also bar the purchase, even in normal markets, of a number of fine issues which sell at unduly high prices in anticipation of greatly increased future earnings."

And later in the same book:

"The stock of a growing company, if purchasable at a suitable price, is obviously preferable to others. No matter how enthusiastic the investor may feel about the prospects of a particular company, however, he should set a limit upon the price that he is willing to pay for such prospects."

That was exactly what I was looking for: buying solid, dependable assets that grow in value over time (although in this case companies rather than houses) and buying them at low prices, just like the housing market of the mid-90s, or the stock market of the early 1990s, 2003 or 2009.

However, while incredibly sensible and useful, Graham's rules were too vague for me to use in practice. My professional background is in computer programming, so I tend to like things to be logically organised into well-defined systems and processes. As the father of Total Quality Management, W. Edwards Deming, once said:

"If you can't describe what you're doing as a process, you don't know what you're doing."

So in 2010 I used that background in computer programming to turn Graham's rules into a complete and systematic investment strategy. My goal was to develop a strategy which would be relatively quick and simple to follow, improvable as new lessons were learned along the way, clear, unambiguous, and which could be applied consistently over many years.

Since then I have continued to use and improve on that strategy, and the results of those years of real-world experience are laid out for you in this book.

PART 1.
QUANTITATIVE ANALYSIS
OF COMPANY ACCOUNTS

The first step on the road to building a defensive value portfolio is to find and buy shares in the right sort of companies at the right price. The key to finding suitable companies is to look at their accounts, because that's where the most important information is.

This initial analysis of company accounts will cover many different areas, but our primary focus will be on measuring growth, quality, profitability and indebtedness. After that we'll turn to some long-term valuation metrics which we can use to decide whether the shares are currently good value or not.

This quantitative analysis should not take too long in practice as our goal at this stage is simply to decide whether or not a company is worth looking at in more detail. After performing these calculations we can then either:

1. Throw the company into the metaphorical bin because it's not the sort right of company

2. Add it to a watch list because it's a good company but the share price is currently too high, or

3. Continue on to a more detailed analysis because the company appears, at first glance, to have a good combination of defensiveness and value.

Part 1 takes you through this process.

CHAPTER 1.

Profitable Dividends

"Each company should have a long record of continuous dividend payments."

BENJAMIN GRAHAM

When I first start looking at a company I like to get the ball rolling with a few simple checks on its dividend history and the earnings upon which those dividends depend. Although defensive value investing isn't necessarily an income-focused approach, dividends do make up the backbone of the strategy.

To make sure we're all on the same page, here's a definition:

> Dividends are cash payments which companies make to their shareholders. Dividends are usually paid out of surplus cash which the company cannot put to good use internally. The dividend is typically quoted in pence per share, where it's known as dividend per share (DPS).

There are several reasons why dividends are central to my approach and why the process of analysing a company begins with them. The most important reasons are:

1. **Efficient capital allocation** – A company should only retain cash generated from its operations if that cash is required to

run the existing business, or if that cash can be invested (in new factories or new equipment for example) at an attractive rate of return. Cash that cannot be deployed in those ways should be returned to shareholders as a dividend. With companies that don't pay a dividend there is a greater risk that the retained cash will be used to expand the CEO's empire rather than maximise returns for shareholders.

2. **Commitment and accountability** – Companies that have a progressive dividend policy have made a promise to investors that they will maintain or grow the dividend each year. This provides a public and very concrete goal for the company's management to achieve. Of course this promise can be broken, but on average dividend commitments do help companies to perform better.

3. **A helpful yardstick** – A progressive dividend gives investors a gauge for the long-term progress of a company. While earnings and to some extent revenues bounce around from year to year, a progressive dividend can give a good indication of the underlying growth rate of a company.

4. **A cash income** – Perhaps the most obvious benefit of dividends is that they are a form of cash income. For those investors who are after an income, either today or in the future, dividends are an excellent way to receive that income without having to sell any shares.

A long history of dividend payments

The logic behind Benjamin Graham's rule on dividends quoted at the start of this chapter is simple. If investors want to buy companies that are likely to pay a consistent dividend in the future, the best place to find such companies is among those that have paid a consistent dividend in the past.

Therefore I look for companies that have paid a dividend consistently over a long period, which I define as ten years. This leads me to this first of many rules of thumb that make up the defensive value approach.

Defensive value rule of thumb

Only invest in a company if it paid a dividend in every one of the last ten years.

I don't mind the odd missing interim or final dividend, as long as some sort of dividend was paid in every year. If there is a year in that ten year period in which no dividends were paid then the company goes straight into my metaphorical wastepaper bin.

It is important to remember that a consistent dividend record is not a magic bullet, because dividend payments are not guaranteed. No matter how good a company's track record, you can never be sure that the dividend won't be cut or suspended at some point in the next few years.

The banking crisis of 2007-2009 was a good example of this. A whole group of companies that were thought to be safe – i.e. the big banks – turned out to be anything but. The banks suspended their dividends, in some cases for several years.

Unfortunately, dividend cuts are a fact of life. If you invest for long enough in dividend-paying companies you will see a dividend cut in your portfolio at some point. However, this is not a reason to abandon the approach.

Instead, the risks of seeing a dividend cut can be reduced by looking at a range of additional factors such as profitability, debt levels and cyclicality. As a last line of defence, your portfolio should be widely diversified across many different companies, which will reduce the impact of the occasional dividend cut when it occurs (we'll cover each of these points in detail later on).

Finding ten years of data

There are various ways you can get hold of a company's financial data for the past ten years. The obvious place to look would be the annual results, but that approach is very time consuming and any per share data, such as dividend per share, will not have been adjusted for share splits or share consolidations.

Share splits and consolidations basically change the number of shares a company has and the price of each share, but they don't affect the value of each shareholder's holdings. However, they do affect per share figures such as dividends and earnings per share, which means that per share figures from older annual and interim results have to be adjusted to take account of the change.

You could do this by hand, but my preferred approach is to get the ten years of data from a provider such as Morningstar or SharePad, at least initially, and to supplement that with the company's official results documents if I decide to get into a more detailed analysis.

You can find a list of data sources and other useful resources in the appendix.

From now on I'll assume you have access to all the required financial data, so let's move on and analyse the dividend record of one of my recent holdings.

The dividend history of Petrofac (PFC)

Petrofac is a FTSE 250-listed company operating in the Oil Equipment, Services & Distribution sector. It is involved in the construction, maintenance and operation of oil and gas facilities worldwide. Up to its 2014 annual results it had the dividend record shown in Table 1.1.

Year	Dividend per share (p)
2005	0.99
2006	4.24
2007	7.52
2008	15.36
2009	21.35
2010	27.33
2011	33.93
2012	41.85
2013	40.35
2014	42.73

Table 1.1: Petrofac's dividend record through ten years to 2014

Looking for dividend payments in every one of the last ten years is a pretty simple test. Either a company made a dividend payment in every year or it didn't. In Petrofac's case it did.

A long history of positive earnings

Of course dividends don't appear out of thin air. A company first has to generate revenues and profits because without profits there can be no sustainable dividends, and without revenues there can be no profits.

Let's nail down some earnings-related terminology:

- **Revenues** – For our purposes this is the total amount of money coming into a company in return for the provision of goods and services, typically over one year. It can be quoted as a total amount in millions of pounds or in pence per share.

- **Pre-tax profit** – This is revenues minus expenses. It is usually quoted as a total amount in millions of pounds. Profit is also a general term which can be used to mean positive earnings (earnings are defined below), in the same way that a loss means negative earnings.

- **Post-tax profit** – This is pre-tax profit minus taxes and is usually quoted as a total amount in millions of pounds.

- **Basic earnings per share (EPS)** – This is post-tax profit per share, usually quoted in pence and usually just called earnings per share. It is the most important financial metric for many investors and is the earnings part of the price to earnings ratio (PE).

- **Adjusted EPS** – This is basic EPS with one-off income and expense items removed. One-off items can be things like income from the disposal of an asset (such as a building or delivery truck) or an expense such as redundancy and legal costs after a plant closure. The idea is to get a better picture of the company's core or underlying earnings by removing the effects of income and expenses that are unlikely to occur every year. This is not an official accounting number as each company has its own interpretation of what is and isn't a one-off item, so it can be difficult to compare one company to the next.

- **Normalised EPS** – This is a standardised version of adjusted EPS which is available on various investment websites such as SharePad, Morningstar and Stockopedia. However, it is not shown in company annual reports and is not an official accounting number.

Personally I use normalised EPS because it is standardised and gives me a better picture of how the underlying company is performing. **When I mention earnings or earnings per share throughout the rest of the book you should assume I mean the normalised version.** If you are going to get your accounting data from each company's annual reports rather than from investment websites you will have to use basic or adjusted earnings per share in place of the normalised version.

When I look at a company's earnings I'm looking for a long history of profits (i.e. positive earnings per share), rather than a company which generates losses (i.e. negative earnings per share) every few years. However, unlike my dividend rule of thumb which says that no company will be considered if it failed to pay a dividend in one year, I don't automatically rule out companies that made a loss at some point in the last ten years.

My thinking here is that while a good company should be able to pay a dividend even when times are tough, the same isn't necessarily true for earnings. With dividends, a good company will have a cash buffer that it can dip into occasionally, but no such buffer exists for earnings. This means that sometimes even very good companies can make the occasional loss.

Having said that, a company which regularly loses money is unlikely to be a suitable investment. I don't want to be overly restrictive, so I'm willing to accept companies that occasionally make losses, as long as the losses are not too frequent or too large.

Overall, companies should have earned more in the last ten years than they paid out in dividends. That at least gives me some confidence that their dividend is sustainable.

Calculating the ten-year dividend cover ratio

The ratio between earnings and dividends is called dividend cover. A dividend cover of more than one means that earnings for the period exceeded dividends paid. Most investors calculate dividend cover for the latest year only, but as with the dividend track record, I prefer to measure it over a ten-year period. The calculation for ten-year dividend cover is:

ten-year dividend cover = ten-year total EPS / ten-year total DPS

The first rule of thumb for earnings is therefore:

Defensive value rule of thumb

Only invest in a company if its ten-year dividend cover is greater than 1.

Let's turn to the real world and see how these concepts can be applied to another of my recent holdings.

Mitie Group's long-term dividend cover

Mitie is a FTSE 250-listed company operating in the Support Services sector. Its main business is the supply of outsourced services to other companies, such as cleaning, security and pest control. It has paid a dividend in every one of the last ten years, so it's definitely a candidate for further analysis.

To check its long-term dividend cover we'll need its earnings and dividends for the last ten years, which you can see in Table 1.2.

Year	Normalised earnings per share (p)	Dividend per share (p)
2005	9.42	3.40
2006	10.31	2.40
2007	11.45	5.10
2008	13.57	6.00
2009	16.25	6.90
2010	18.40	7.80
2011	21.05	9.00
2012	20.43	9.60
2013	22.31	10.30
2014	24.70	11.00
Total	167.89	71.50

Table 1.2: Mitie's dividends and earnings per share, 2005-2014

Mitie's earnings record shows an unbroken string of profits during the period. Although I'm not put off by the occasional loss, I do prefer to see unbroken profits like Mitie's.

As for the company's ten-year dividend cover, it's clear just from looking at the numbers that the dividend is well covered in every year, so obviously the ratio is above 1. However, I still think it's worth calculating the ratio anyway as it's a good habit to get into. For Mitie the calculation goes like this:

ten-year dividend per share total = 71.50p

ten-year earnings per share total = 167.89p

ten-year dividend cover = 167.89p / 71.50p = 2.3

Mitie's ten-year dividend cover over the ten years to 2014 was 2.3, which is obviously well above my minimum of 1, so Mitie easily ticks that particular box.

In the next chapter we'll turn to the subject of measuring a company's growth, but first here's a quick summary of the rules we have covered so far.

Rules of thumb for profitable dividends

- Only invest in a company if it paid a dividend in every one of the last ten years.
- Only invest in a company if its ten-year dividend cover is greater than 1.

CHAPTER 2.

Consistent Growth

"The stock of a growing company, if purchasable at a suitable price, is obviously preferable to others."

Benjamin Graham

A company that consistently makes a profit and consistently pays a dividend is a good partial definition of a defensive company, but there are other things to look for too. Thanks to inflation, unless a company can grow its earnings and dividends over time then in real terms the value of its economic output will fall. This means that in addition to consistent profits and dividend payments, I always look for consistent growth.

Growth can be broken down into two components – quality and speed – and I will look at both of these in turn in this chapter.

Measuring long-term growth quality

One simple way to measure the quality of a company's growth is to count how many times its dividend went up in the last ten years. The more often the dividend went up, the higher quality the company's growth was.

Of course measuring a company's growth quality purely by looking at its dividend growth is overly simplistic, but this is just the beginning. We can also apply this idea to revenues and earnings. By combining the frequency of growth across revenues, earnings and dividends it is possible to calculate a reasonably robust measure of the quality of a company's growth, which I call the **growth quality** score.

Measuring growth quality across revenues, earnings and dividends

It's a bit unusual to measure the quality of a company's growth in this way, but there are good reasons for doing so. Many companies are able to progressively increase their dividends for a long time, and progressive dividend growth is what the majority of defensive investors look for. However, if a company's revenues and earnings are volatile from one year to the next then there is a greater chance of a problem, of one sort or another, at some point down the road.

On the other hand, companies which can steadily increase their revenues and earnings each year, as well as their dividend, generally have more predictable and defensive businesses. This means their dividends may be safer, all else being equal. This stability can also make it easier to value these companies and to forecast what might happen to them in the future, relative to more volatile companies.

Before I get into the details of exactly how we can calculate this growth quality score, I just want to explain why the calculation differs between financial companies and non-financial companies.

Book value as an alternative to revenue for financial companies

Financial companies, such as banks and insurers, are a special case. Instead of revenue, banks often refer to net interest income, while insurance companies use terms like net earned premium or insurance revenue. This can make things rather complicated, so instead of revenue I use book value (often called shareholders' equity) as the top line measure of a financial company's progress.

Here's a short definition of book value:

> Book value is a balance sheet item equal to total assets minus total liabilities. It is also known as net asset value, shareholders' equity or total equity.

For banks, book value is (very approximately) the difference between loans (which are an asset from the bank's point of view) and deposits (which are a liability). Banks primarily make a profit from the difference between what it costs them to borrow (the interest they pay on deposits) and what they earn from lending those deposits out (the interest they receive on loans). Generally speaking, an increase in book value means a bank is taking in more deposits and making more loans, which in turn means it has the potential to produce larger earnings and dividends. It's similar to how an increase in revenues for non-financial companies creates the potential for more earnings and more dividends.

The same sort of story applies to insurance companies. In their case book value can be thought of (again, very approximately) as the difference between insurance premiums that have been put aside to cover the cost of future claims (which are an asset) and the expected costs of those future claims (which are liabilities). Again, generally speaking, an increase in book value means an insurance company has taken in more premiums in order to cover more insurance risk, which in turn means it has the potential to produce larger earnings and dividends.

As with growth quality for revenues, earnings and dividends, calculating the growth quality of book value for financial companies is just a case of noting down how many times their book value went up over the last ten years. **From here onwards, if I mention revenues then take that to mean book value in the case of financial companies**.

Taking account of losses

If a company repeatedly generates losses then it is unlikely to be a good candidate for investment, so the final element in the growth quality score is losses. The more often a company loses money the lower its growth quality score should be. We can take account of this by simply reducing the growth quality score by one for every year in the last ten in which a loss was made.

Calculating growth quality

To calculate growth quality you'll need revenues, earnings per share and dividends per share going back over the last ten years. You should already have the earnings and dividend figures from calculating the long-term dividend cover.

Now we can take the following steps:

1. Count how many times the company made a loss in the last ten years

2. Count how many times revenues went up in the last ten years

3. Count how many times earnings per share went up in the last ten years

4. Count how many times dividends per share went up in the last ten years

5. Add up the number of revenue, earnings and dividend increases and then subtract the number of losses

6. Convert to a percentage

Don't worry if that looks complicated as we'll be working through an example shortly. And also don't forget there are spreadsheets in the appendix which can do the calculations for you.

Once again I have a rule of thumb for growth quality, which should help to rule out companies whose growth is too volatile to be considered defensive.

Defensive value rule of thumb

Only invest in a company if its growth quality is above 50%.

Let's have a look at how the growth quality score works in the real world with an example.

Centrica's growth quality

Centrica is a FTSE 100-listed integrated energy company involved in the generation, transmission and delivery of energy to businesses and consumers in the UK and North America. In the UK most people will know it through its most famous brand, British Gas.

Table 2.1 shows Centrica's revenues, earnings and dividends up to its 2014 annual results.

Year	Revenue (£m)	Earnings per share (p)	Dividend per share (p)
2005	13,448	15.30	9.30
2006	16,403	17.16	9.93
2007	16,272	27.72	11.57
2008	20,872	3.41	12.63
2009	21,963	23.74	12.80
2010	22,423	43.11	14.30
2011	22,824	19.32	15.40
2012	23,942	36.57	16.40
2013	26,571	37.57	17.00
2014	29,408	5.53	13.50
No. of increases	8	6	8

Table 2.1: Centrica's results for ten years to 2014

I don't think it's very easy to get a feel for how stable Centrica's results are just by looking at a table of numbers like this. Its revenues go up quite steadily, but earnings per share seem to go down almost as often as they go up. This confusion is precisely the sort of problem the growth quality score is designed to solve, or at least reduce.

By converting all those revenue, earnings and dividend figures into a single growth quality number it becomes much easier to understand how stable Centrica has been; that in turn makes it much easier to compare Centrica to other companies.

I'll calculate Centrica's growth quality score step by step to show you how it works:

1. **Count how many times the company made a loss in the last ten years.** Looking at the table there are no years with negative earnings per share, therefore the number of losses in the period was zero.

2. **Count how many times revenues went up in the last ten years.** Out of a maximum of nine possible increases, Centrica achieved eight.

3. **Count how many times earnings per share went up in the last ten years.** Out of a maximum of nine possible increases, Centrica achieved six.

4. **Count how many times dividends per share went up in the last ten years.** Out of a maximum of nine possible increases, Centrica achieved eight.

5. **Add up the revenue, earnings and dividend increases and then subtract the number of losses.** Revenue increases = 8, EPS increases = 6, DPS increases = 8 and losses (negative EPS) = 0

6. **Adding those up gives**:

growth quality as a number = 8 + 6 + 8 – 0 = 22

7. **Convert to a percentage**

growth quality = 22 / 27 × 100 = 81%

Note that the growth quality as a number is divided by 27 to turn it into a percentage as 27 is the maximum possible score, i.e. a company with growth quality as a number of 27 would have a growth quality score of 100%.

One thing you may have noticed is that Centrica cut its dividend in 2014. Although many income-focused investors like to avoid companies that have a dividend cut in their past, I am less put off by dividend cuts and do not automatically rule out companies solely on that basis. However, it does count as a negative factor in my analysis.

Measuring the long-term growth rate

Benjamin Graham said that a growing company is preferable to others, which seems obvious enough. I would go one step further and say that a high-growth company is preferable to a low-growth company (all else being equal, of course).

In order to differentiate between the hares and the tortoises I use a measure of growth which is:

1. Broadly based, so that it reflects the company's overall growth rate as much as possible, and

2. Focused on long-term growth, rather than growth over just the last few years.

Long-term revenue, earnings and dividend growth

As with growth quality, I measure a company's growth rate by combining the growth of its revenues, earnings and dividends over a ten-year period. The idea is to use the past to estimate the company's sustainable future growth rate, which will always be impossible to know exactly.

One problem with measuring growth is that it depends to a great extent on which years are chosen as the start and end points. Unusually high or low earnings at the start or end of the period being measured, for example, will have a major impact on the calculated growth rate.

To get around this problem, Benjamin Graham proposed measuring growth between the average of the oldest three years in a ten-year period and the average of the latest three years. By doing that the revenues, earnings or dividends in any one year become less important and the general change over a number of years becomes more important.

It is exactly that sort of sustained change in revenues, earnings and dividends that I'm looking for, which is why I have incorporated this technique into the strategy. For obvious reasons I call the results of this calculation a company's **growth rate**.

Calculating a company's growth rate

Using the ten-year figures we've already written down for revenues, earnings per share and dividends per share, the steps for calculating a company's growth rate are:

1. Calculate the average revenues for the oldest three-year period

2. Calculate the average revenues for the latest three-year period

3. Calculate revenue growth:

revenue growth =
(new average revenues / old average revenues) – 1 x 100%

4. Repeat steps 2 to 4 for earnings and dividends per share to calculate earnings growth and dividend growth

5. Calculate overall growth as the average of revenue, earnings and dividend growth:

overall growth =
(revenue growth + earnings growth + dividend growth) / 3

6. The growth rate is the annual rate of growth required to produce the company's overall growth over that period, expressed as a percentage. There are two ways to calculate it:

approximate growth rate = overall growth / 7

accurate growth rate = $((1 + \text{overall growth})^{1/7} - 1)$

If you're wondering why the number 7 appears in the growth rate calculations, it's because the growth rate is measured over the seven-year period between the old three-year average and the new three-year average.

The approximate version of the growth rate is much easier to calculate by hand and is probably good enough as long as you use it consistently and don't swap back and forth between the two versions. However, the accurate version can be calculated for you if you use a spreadsheet, and so for the rest of the book **you should assume I'm always talking about the accurate version of the growth rate**.

For growth rate I use a rule of thumb to exclude companies that fail to grow faster than inflation (currently targeted at 2% by the Bank of England).

Defensive value rule of thumb

Only invest in a company if its growth rate is above 2%.

Let's see how this one works in the real world.

Admiral Group's growth rate

Admiral Group is one of the UK's leading car insurers and has grown rapidly for many years. To drive that growth forwards it is looking to international markets, as well as house insurance in the UK. As it's an insurance company its growth rate is calculated using book value rather than revenues (I have used book value per share because it was available from my data provider, but you could just as legitimately use total book value from the annual results). Table 2.2 shows how the company has performed over the last ten years.

Year	Book value per share (p)	Earnings per share (p)	Dividend per share (p)
2005	70.00	32.90	29.60
2006	84.05	39.86	32.40
2007	90.71	48.60	43.80
2008	104.43	54.90	52.50
2009	112.98	59.00	57.50
2010	130.55	72.20	68.10
2011	145.47	81.70	75.60
2012	167.80	94.90	90.60
2013	187.69	104.40	99.50
2014	204.52	102.80	98.40
Total growth	128.8%	148.9%	172.7%

Table 2.2: Admiral's results for the ten years to 2014

You can get a sense of how fast Admiral has grown by looking at its 2005 book value, earnings and dividends per share compared with the values for 2014. All of them have more or less tripled in that time so the company is definitely growing quickly. However, as with growth quality, it will be much easier to understand Admiral's growth rate and compare it to other companies if the mass of figures in Table 2.2 is first converted into a single number.

Following the steps outlined previously, here is the calculation for Admiral's growth rate:

1. **Calculate the average revenues for the oldest three-year period.** Book value per share (rather than revenues) for 2005, 2006 and 2007 was 70.00, 84.05 and 90.71 pence respectively, so:

old average revenue = (70.00 + 84.05 + 90.71) / 3 = 81.58 pence

2. **Calculate the average revenues for the latest three-year period.** Book value per share for 2012, 2013 and 2014 was 167.80, 187.69 and 204.52 pence respectively, so:

new average revenue = (167.80 + 187.69 + 204.52) / 3 = 186.67 pence

3. **Calculate revenue growth:**

revenue growth = (186.67 / 81.58) − 1 = 1.288 × 100% = 128.8%

4. **Repeat steps 1 to 3 for earnings and dividends per share to calculate EPS growth and DPS growth**

EPS growth rate:

i.   EPS for 2005, 2006 and 2007 was 32.90, 39.86 and 48.60 pence respectively, so:

old average EPS = (32.90 + 39.86 + 48.60) / 3 = 40.45p

ii. EPS for 2012, 2013 and 2014 was 94.90, 104.40 and 102.80 pence respectively, so:

new average EPS = (94.90 + 104.40 + 102.80) / 3 = 100.70p

iii. Calculate EPS growth:

EPS growth = (100.70 / 40.45) – 1 × 100 = 148.9%

DPS growth rate:

i.   DPS for 2005, 2006 and 2007 was 29.60, 32.40 and 43.80 pence respectively, so:

old average DPS = (29.60 + 32.40 + 43.80) / 3 = 35.27p

ii. DPS for 2012, 2013 and 2014 was 90.60, 99.50 and 98.40 pence respectively, so:

new average DPS = (90.60 + 99.50 + 98.40) / 3 = 96.17p

iii. Calculate EPS growth:

DPS growth = (96.17 / 35.27) – 1 × 100 = 172.7%

5. **Calculate overall growth as the average of revenue, earnings and dividend growth:**

overall growth = (128.8% + 148.9% + 172.7%) / 3 = 150.1%

6. **Growth rate is the annual rate of growth required to produce the company's overall growth over that period, expressed as a percentage. There are two ways to calculate it:**

approximate growth rate = 150.1% / 7 = 21.4%

accurate growth rate = $((1 + 150.1\%)^{1/7} - 1) = 14.0\%$

So Admiral produced overall growth for that period of 150.1%, giving it an annualised growth rate of 14% per year.

This is well above my 2% rule of thumb minimum and well above inflation for the period as well. On that basis I think it's reasonable to call Admiral a high-growth company.

Surprisingly, not all growth is good, so in the next chapter I'll explain how I look for companies that are highly profitable as well, since high profitability is one of the most important traits of high quality companies.

Here's a summary of the rules of thumb we have covered in this chapter.

Rules of thumb for consistent growth

- Only invest in a company if its growth quality is above 50%.
- Only invest in a company if its growth rate is above 2%.

CHAPTER 3.

High Profitability

"By itself, [earnings per share] says nothing about economic performance. To evaluate that, we must know how much total capital – debt and equity – was needed to produce these earnings."

WARREN BUFFETT

Profitability is an important concept because it indicates the sort of return a company could get on any earnings which it does not pay out to shareholders as a dividend. High profitability is also frequently associated with companies that have strong competitive advantages.

In this chapter I'll outline how I measure a company's long-term profitability and some of the important differences between profitability for insurance companies and banks compared to other companies.

If you're not familiar with the concept of profitability or why it can be a good way to see if a company has a competitive advantage, have a read through the following – somewhat unlikely – story.

Profitability in competitive markets

Imagine that one day you wake up and decide to run a lemonade stand. The first thing you do is buy a stand, an advertising banner, cups, lemons and a little sugar. After that you hire an inexpensive teenager to make and sell the lemonade.

The total cost of the company's fixed capital (things the business will own for a long time such as the advertising banner and lemonade stand) plus its working capital (things the business will own for a short time such as cups, lemons and sugar) is £1000. Together these make up the company's capital employed, i.e. the total amount of money tied up in the business.

In this story your lemonade stand is the only one in the area and as such it has a monopoly on lemonade sold locally. This means you have 100% of the market and can optimise your price in order to maximise profits.

In the first year you make £10,000 profit, which is a 1000% return on your investment, i.e. a 1000% return on capital employed in the business (otherwise known as ROCE).

A 1000% return means that your business is incredibly profitable. If it were really plausible to do this then everybody would be running lemonade stands and achieving a 1000% annual return on their investment. However, nothing attracts attention like money and a lemonade stand with a return on capital employed of 1000% is going to attract a lot of attention. In no time at all you would have competition, and lots of it.

As you start your second year in the lemonade business nine new lemonade stands appear on the same street as yours. Demand hasn't grown but supply has, so your company will face a drop in sales. Because your competitors' lemonade is comparable to yours, your market share falls to just 10% of the market (there are now ten lemonade stands in total and you each achieve an equal market share). Your annual revenues and profits drop dramatically. That would be bad enough, but your problems are not over yet.

Some of the other lemonade stand owners decide to lower their prices below yours in order to win additional market share. As a result of all this competition the price of a cup of lemonade is eventually driven down to the point where your profits in year two are just £100. In other words, your return on capital employed (your initial £1000 investment) is now just 10% and you begin to feel that it is barely worth running a lemonade stand at all.

In this scenario there are two ways your business can survive:

1. Run your business more efficiently and cheaply than everyone else. This will allow you to make a profit when prices are so low that others are making a loss.

2. Make your lemonade unique. If you can sell lemonade that is in some way different and preferable to everyone else's lemonade you may not have to compete with them on price.

This is the creative destruction of capitalism at its best, pushing up the quality of products and services while pushing down the price.

If the lemonade stand market becomes so competitive that nobody can make a decent profit, i.e. a decent return on capital employed, no new stands will be set up. Entrepreneurs and investors will simply choose to start other businesses with higher returns instead.

The same should be true of existing stand owners as well. If their returns fall significantly below the amount they could get from an equally risky business (perhaps bubble gum stands are more profitable at this point in time), then the economically rational thing to do would be to sell their lemonade stand and invest the proceeds into that higher return business. As competitors leave the lemonade market supply will dry up, prices may rise due to the reduced competition and return on capital employed for the remaining businesses might start to head back up again.

The result of this whole process is that most companies return something close to the opportunity cost of their capital, where opportunity cost is the return investors could get from doing something else with their capital that entails a similar degree of risk.

A good measure of opportunity cost for relatively defensive investors is the long-run return on the UK stock market as a whole. Historically, the UK market has produced a total return after inflation of about 5% per year over the long term, so any company which consistently produces returns on capital employed below about 7% (based on a 5% real return plus 2% expected inflation) is either operating in a very competitive market or has a very weak competitive position.

The importance of high profitability

Profitability matters because companies that have low profitability are, typically, less defensive than companies that are highly profitable.

Low profitability companies typically have:

1. **A harder time growing** – This is because their profits are small relative to their assets (e.g. factories, machinery or vehicles) and so they have to reinvest more of their profits to build new factories or buy new machinery.

2. **Little margin for error** – They have thin profit margins and small profits that can be wiped out by any number of minor problems which, in turn, may put the dividend at risk.

3. **No competitive advantage** – They are susceptible to competitors who may find better or cheaper ways of serving their customers.

High profitability companies typically have:

1. **An easier time growing** – Their profits are larger relative to their assets so it takes a smaller portion of their profits to build or buy new productive assets.

2. **A wider margin for error** – They have fatter profit margins and larger profits that may be hurt by minor problems but are less likely to be wiped out, making it easier to maintain dividend payments.

3. **Strong competitive advantages** – They are less susceptible to competition as competitive advantages make it difficult to compete with them (I cover competitive advantages in much more detail later).

Put simply, profitability is an important indicator of the defensiveness and competitiveness of a company, which is why it is one of my key metrics and the topic of this chapter.

Measuring return on capital employed

As I mentioned in the lemonade stand story, return on capital employed (ROCE) is a useful measure of profitability. ROCE can be measured in a few different ways, but the typical approach is to take returns to be operating profits while capital employed is made up of fixed assets and working capital (which is current assets minus current liabilities).

The reason operating profits are used is that it keeps the ratio focused on the operations of the business, i.e. the operating profits are being compared to the operating capital of the business. Factors that relate to how that operating capital was paid for, such as how much the company has borrowed or how much it pays in debt interest, are ignored.

However, I prefer to use net profits in the ratio, i.e. profits after interest and tax, precisely because it takes into account any interest the company is paying on its debts. This net return on capital employed is an unusual approach, and if you're an accountant it may annoy you, so you're welcome to use operating profits when calculating ROCE instead.

Since I like to look at things over the long term I don't measure ROCE just for last year. Instead I focus on its median value (i.e. middle value) over the last ten years. I think this provides a much clearer picture of the sort of returns a company is likely to produce while I'm owning it, which is usually a period of between one and ten years. For the sake of simplicity I'll refer to this ten-year median net return on capital employed as a company's **profitability**.

Profitability for non-financial companies

By non-financial companies I mean companies that are not banks and insurers. I make this distinction because ROCE is not a useful ratio for financial companies. The structure of their balance sheets means that working capital isn't a useful concept so for financial companies the calculation is slightly different. I'll cover profitability for non-financial companies here and then look at financial companies afterwards.

To calculate profitability for non-financial companies you'll need the following figures for the last ten years:

1. **Post-tax profit** – You can find this on the income statement. I prefer to use normalised post-tax profit, which uses the same adjustments as normalised EPS. If you don't have access to normalised figures through your data provider you can use adjusted or reported post-tax profits from the company's annual results.

2. **Fixed assets** – The company's long-term assets, which you can find on the balance sheet.

3. **Current assets** – The company's short-term assets, which you can find on the balance sheet.

4. **Current liabilities** – The company's short-term liabilities, which you can find on the balance sheet.

Once you have those figures, work through the following steps (using a spreadsheet will make this much quicker and easier):

5. Calculate the capital employed within the business for each year as:

capital employed = fixed assets + current assets – current liabilities

6. Calculate net ROCE for each year as:

net ROCE = (post-tax profit / capital employed) × 100

7. Take profitability to be the median net ROCE for the period, i.e. the middle value if the results were all aligned in ascending order.

Given that an index tracker is likely to provide a long-term return of about 7% a year, I use the following rule of thumb for profitability.

Defensive value rule of thumb

Only invest in a company if its profitability is above 7%.

In addition, higher profitability is better than lower, assuming everything else is equal.

Let's take that theory and apply it to another example from my recent holdings.

British American Tobacco's profitability

British American Tobacco (BAT), as the name suggests, is a FTSE 100 company with a long history in the tobacco industry. It owns brands such as Dunhill and Rothmans and is investing in and researching electronic cigarettes as regulation on smoking gets ever tighter.

To calculate net return on capital employed we'll need post-tax profit and capital employed (fixed assets plus current assets minus current liabilities), which you can see in Table 3.1, along with the net ROCE value for each year.

Year	Post-tax profit (£m)	Capital employed (£m)	Net ROCE
2005	2,021	13,215	15.3%
2006	2,037	13,323	15.3%
2007	2,238	14,210	15.7%
2008	2,611	18,673	14.0%
2009	3,122	19,698	15.8%
2010	3,487	20,215	17.2%
2011	3,869	19,272	20.1%
2012	4,011	19,185	20.9%

Year	Post-tax profit (£m)	Capital employed (£m)	Net ROCE
2013	4,161	18,445	22.6%
2014	3,660	17,398	21.0%

Table 3.1: British American Tobacco's results to 2014

Here's the calculation for British American Tobacco's profitability, step by step:

1. **Calculate the capital employed within the business for each year.** I'll just work through this step for 2005 as each year will be the same but with different figures. In 2005 BAT had fixed assets of £13,147m, current assets of £5,904m and current liabilities of £5,836m:

2005 capital employed = £13,147m + £5,904m – £5,836m = £13,215m

2. **Calculate net ROCE for each year.** Again, I'll just run through this for 2005. In 2005 BAT had net profits of £2,021m and capital employed of £13,215m:

2005 net ROCE = (£2,021m / £13,215m) × 100% = 15.3%

3. **Take profitability to be the median net ROCE for the period, i.e. the middle value if the results were all aligned in ascending order.** After listing the net ROCE figures for the ten years in ascending order, the middle two values are 15.8% and 17.2%. The median for the period is the average of those two, which is 16.5%.

That means British American Tobacco's profitability for 2005 to 2014 is 16.5%.

My rule of thumb minimum is 7% so of course that test is easily passed. Warren Buffett is said to prefer companies with *pre-tax* returns on capital of at least 15%, so British American Tobacco's score puts it well into that territory given that 16.5% is a *post-tax* figure.

Profitability for financial companies

For financial companies such as banks and insurers I use return on equity (ROE) instead of net ROCE. ROE is the ratio between post-tax profits and shareholders' equity (book value), which is equal to total assets minus total liabilities. I'll go into the balance sheets of financial companies in more detail in the next chapter, so for now I'll just say that ROE makes more sense than ROCE when calculating profitability for these companies.

The calculation is almost the same as before, except in this case you won't need to find the figures for fixed assets, current assets or current liabilities. Instead you'll need:

- **Shareholders' equity** – Also known as total equity, book value or net asset value; can be found on the balance sheet.

In fact you should already have this data as shareholders' equity (i.e. book value) is used in the calculation of both growth rate and growth quality for financial companies.

To calculate profitability for financial companies the steps are:

1. Calculate ROE for each year as:

ROE = (post-tax profit / shareholders' equity) × 100

2. Take profitability to be the median ROE for the period, i.e. the middle value when all the results are placed in ascending order.

3. The rule of thumb for financial company profitability is the same as before (above 7%). However, in addition to return on equity, we will also be measuring the profitability of insurance companies with the combined ratio as well.

The combined ratio for insurance companies

To understand the combined ratio we need to look at the two ways in which insurance companies make their profits:

1. **Underwriting (insurance) profit** – Writing insurance policies where the premium more than covers the expected cost of claims and other expenses.

2. **Investment profit** – Between the time that premiums are collected and the time they are paid out to cover claims (which can be many years), insurance companies invest those premiums and record whatever returns the investment markets provide as a profit (or a loss if the investments do badly).

Generally an insurance company would want to make good profits on both the underwriting and investment sides of its business. However, of the two forms of profit, underwriting profit is the most important because it represents the profit from the company's core insurance business rather than the ups and downs of the investment markets. The combined ratio is how we can measure that underwriting profit.

I'll explain how the combined ratio works with an example.

Imagine an insurance company that receives £100m in car insurance premiums, but expects to have to pay out £105m in claims and £5m in expenses. Under those circumstances it would make an underwriting loss of £10m (£100m premium income minus £105m claims minus £5m expenses).

The scale of this loss can be measured with the combined ratio as the combined ratio is a combination of both the loss ratio (the ratio of claims – known as losses – to premiums) and the expense ratio (the ratio of expenses to premiums).

So in the previous example the company has a loss ratio of 105% (ratio of £105m of claims to £100m of premiums) and an expense ratio of 5% (ratio of £5m of expenses to £100m of premiums) giving a combined ratio of 110%. The company made a £10m underwriting loss and so, as you can see, a combined ratio which is over 100% shows that an insurance company has been losing money on its underwriting activities.

Although most of the time insurance companies will want to make profits on both sides of their businesses, this is not always the case. A good example of this would be the long stock market boom of the 1990s, where many insurance companies were able to make huge profits primarily on the investment side of their business. In fact, investment returns were so good that many were willing to offer insurance for less than the expected cost of claims (in other words to make an underwriting loss) just to get their hands on more premiums which they could then invest in the stock market.

Of course making an underwriting loss every year would be a very bad way to run a business were it not for the fact that the insurance premiums, once collected, can be invested to generate an investment return. Using the previous example, if the £100m of premiums were invested for an annual return of 20% then the £20m investment return would more than offset the £10m underwriting loss. The result would be a net profit. That's basically what a lot of insurance companies were doing during the heady days of the dot-com boom. It's a very risky way to run an insurance business because investment returns can be volatile and profits can quickly turn to losses.

Table 3.2 shows the combined ratios of several leading insurance companies at two separate points in time.

Company	2000	2013
Admiral	Not listed in 2000	89%
Amlin	111%	86%
Aviva	109%	97%
RSA	110%	97%

Table 3.2: Combined ratios for some leading insurance companies

Each company that existed in 2000 was willing to write insurance at an underwriting loss, i.e. the combined ratios are all above 100%. Each ratio in 2000 is around 110%, which means each premium payment of £100 was expected to cost the company around £110 in claims and expenses. The management of each company must have believed that investment returns would more than offset those underwriting losses. Unfortunately for their shareholders, it didn't quite work out that way.

When the stock market fell from 2000 to 2003 each company would have made heavy losses on any equity investments and there would have been no underwriting profits to fall back on.

That's why I insist that any insurance company I invest in has a profitable underwriting business, so that it doesn't have to be overly reliant on risky and volatile investment returns.

My rule of thumb for insurance company profitability checks that over a period of time the company has made a reasonable profit from its underwriting business:

Defensive value rule of thumb

Only invest in an insurance company if its five-year average combined ratio is less than 95%.

The combined ratio isn't used by life insurance companies (insurance companies are usually categorised as life or non-life, as the two markets require substantially different business models), so don't be surprised if you find a company in the life insurance sector which doesn't quote one. However, if the company does have general (non-life) insurance operations as well, as Aviva does, then it probably will quote a figure for the combined ratio. The best approach is to just scan through the annual results to see if the ratio is there. If I can't find a combined ratio in an insurance company's annual results then I'll just measure its profitability with return on equity alone.

Okay that's enough theory; let's work through a couple of examples using a company I have recently been invested in.

Amlin's profitability

Amlin is a FTSE 250-listed reinsurance company (i.e. it provides insurance to insurance companies) that operates primarily through Lloyd's of London, but also has operations abroad. Note that Amlin has recently been taken over and de-listed from the stock market, but that does not change the usefulness of this example.

You can see the relevant figures for Amlin in Table 3.3.

Year	Post-tax profit (£m)	Shareholders' equity (£m)	ROE
2005	140	785	17.9%
2006	268	936	28.6%
2007	354	1,052	33.7%
2008	80	1,216	6.6%
2009	466	1,593	29.2%
2010	236	1,730	13.6%
2011	-137	1,420	-9.7%
2012	266	1,498	17.8%
2013	293	1,679	17.5%
2014	234	1,786	13.1%

Table 3.3: Amlin results to 2014

Let's go ahead and calculate Amlin's profitability:

1. **Calculate ROE for each year**

As before I'll just do this for 2005. All other years follow the same process.

2005 ROE = (£140m / £785m) × 100 = 17.9%

2. **Take profitability to be the median ROE for the period, i.e. the middle value if the results were all aligned in ascending order.**

After sorting Amlin's ROE results into ascending order the middle two values are 17.5% and 17.8%. The median is the average of those two, which is 17.6%.

Despite making a loss in 2011 (due to major earthquakes in New Zealand and Japan), Amlin's profitability is 17.6%, which is very high and a long way clear of my 7% minimum.

As with British American Tobacco, Amlin is an above average company when it comes to long-term profitability.

Amlin's combined ratio

I'll use Amlin again as the example for the combined ratio so that you can see how it performs on a different measure of profitability to ROE.

This time there are almost no calculations to be done – if the company has a combined ratio then it is simply stated in the annual results. All you have to do is search for it and make a note of its value over a five-year period, which you can see for Amlin in Table 3.4.

Year	Combined ratio
2010	89%
2011	108%
2012	89%
2013	86%
2014	89%
Average	92.2%

Table 3.4: Amlin's combined ratio for the five years to 2014

Amlin's average combined ratio over this period is 92.2%, so its underwriting business has been profitable enough to pass my 95% rule of thumb. This is further evidence of the company's strong profitability.

In the next chapter we'll turn from looking at how profitable a company's assets are to how the purchase of those assets has been funded.

For now, here's a summary of the rules of thumb from this chapter.

Rules of thumb for high profitability

- Only invest in a company if its profitability is above 7%.

- Only invest in an insurance company if its five-year average combined ratio is less than 95%.

CHAPTER 4.

Conservative Finances

"Each company selected should be large, prominent, and conservatively financed. Indefinite as these adjectives must be, their general sense is clear."

BENJAMIN GRAHAM

Companies are essentially a collection of assets, such as factories, equipment or cash in the bank, deployed in the pursuit of a common goal (either social, financial or a combination of both). How those assets are financed (such as through short-term credit, longer-term loans or shareholder equity) can have a dramatic effect on both the risks and returns that a company and its investors can expect to see.

As an example of how risks and returns are affected by a company's funding arrangements, imagine a company that borrows £1m at an interest rate of 10% to build a new factory. If that factory is expected to produce an annual return on investment of 15% then taking on debt to build the factory may be a good idea. The £100,000 annual interest expense (10% interest on borrowings of £1m) would be more than offset by the factory's £150,000 annual profit (15% return on investment from the new £1m factory), leaving an additional £50,000 return each year for the company's shareholders.

However, what if the new factory's annual profits fell sharply during an economic downturn, perhaps to just £50,000? In that case the factory's profits have fallen by two-thirds, which is bad enough. But the £100,000 annual interest charge would still have to be paid and so in fact the annual net return, i.e. factory profit minus debt interest, has swung from a £50,000 profit to a £50,000 loss.

When things are going well debt financing can boost returns, but when events take a turn for the worse too much debt can hugely exacerbate even minor declines in profits and quickly turn them into losses.

And it gets worse. In that example, if the company did not have the funds to pay the interest in full the bank may be able to ask for the entire £1m loan back immediately, which would mean either having to sell the factory in a hurry (and probably at a price far below the original £1m), or the company could ask shareholders for additional equity funds via a rights issue to pay back the debt. Neither outcome is likely to be welcomed by shareholders.

That's not to say that having no debt is the best option. There is a sweet spot between having no debt, which is safer but reduces profits, and having too much debt, where profits are boosted but only by taking excessive risk.

In this chapter I'll explain the methods I use to find companies that are operating their finances in that sweet spot.

Conservative finances for non-financial companies

I'll start with non-financial companies because they're relatively straightforward (financial companies such as banks and insurance companies have more complex financing arrangements, which I'll cover shortly).

For the sort of relatively defensive, successful companies I'm interested in, the meaning of conservative financing basically comes down to the amount of money the company has borrowed compared to its ability to pay the interest on those borrowings in both good times and bad.

There are lots of different ways to examine this. Two of the most popular are:

1. Interest cover, typically defined as the ratio between operating profits and interest payments.

2. Net debt to EBITDA, where net debt is total borrowings minus cash and EBITDA is earnings before interest, tax, depreciation and amortisation (amortisation is effectively depreciation applied to intangible assets).

Personally I don't use either of these methods because they rely on earnings from a single year, typically the most recent year. I think it makes more sense to compare debt or interest to a company's average earnings over a number of years, because earnings in a single year are volatile and unreliable. Using average earnings should produce a ratio which is more reliable and robust than one which depends on the earnings of a single year.

I also prefer to use profit after tax rather than EBIT or EBITDA. Post-tax profit is also post-interest, so companies that have large debts, or which pay high interest rates on borrowed money, will have lower post-tax profits than otherwise. Any debt ratio based on post-tax profits will look even worse for these companies and that's exactly what I want.

Taking those ideas into account, I use a debt ratio which is simply the company's total borrowings (where borrowings refers to interest-bearing debts) divided by its most recent five-year average post-tax profit. Rather predictably I have named this the **debt ratio.**

I do have a rule of thumb associated with the debt ratio, but the exact amount of debt I allow will depend on whether the company operates in a cyclical or defensive industry.

Differences between cyclical and defensive companies

In simple terms, cyclical industries have cycles of boom and bust while defensive industries don't, or at least they experience these cycles to a much smaller extent. During boom periods cyclical company profits grow year after year, but when boom turns to bust those profits can shrink dramatically and frequently turn to losses. As we saw in the example at the start of the chapter, a company's cyclicality is an important factor when considering how much debt it can conservatively carry, because debt interest payments should be sustainable through both the peak and trough of each industry cycle.

The unpredictable nature of cyclical company profits means that the maximum amount of debt I'll allow for those companies is less than it is for defensive companies whose profits are, on the whole, more predictable.

Now that we've established that, let's have a look at how I decide whether a company operates in a cyclical or defensive industry.

Is a company defensive or cyclical?

In short, to determine if a company is defensive or cyclical I turn to the Capita Dividend Monitor, which is a quarterly newsletter outlining dividend developments in the UK market. It has a list of the official FTSE sectors, with each defined as either defensive or cyclical. Each company exists in one FTSE sector and you can find out which one by looking at the London Stock Exchange website (www.londonstockexchange.com), or data providers such as ShareScope.

Unfortunately, different data providers sometimes use different sector definitions, but I stick to the official ones, which are called the Industry Classification Benchmark (ICB) sectors. In some cases judgment is required to decide if a company really is defensive or cyclical, but in most cases the Capita Dividend Monitor definitions are good enough. You can see the ICB sectors and their defensive/cyclical definition from the Capita Dividend Monitor in Table 4.1.

Defensive	Cyclical
Beverages	Banks
Electricity	Chemicals
Food & Drug Retailers	Electronic & Electrical Equipment
Food Producers	Financial Services
Health Care Equipment & Services	General Industrials
Mobile Telecommunications	General Retailers
Tobacco	Industrial Transportation
	Life Insurance

Defensive	Cyclical
	Media
	Oil & Gas Producers
	Oil Equipment, Services & Distribution
	Real Estate Investment & Services
	Software & Computer Services
	Support Services
	Technology Hardware & Equipment
	Travel & Leisure

Table 4.1: Defensive and cyclical sectors as defined in the Capita Dividend Monitor

Calculating the debt ratio

We now have all of the basic ideas which go into the debt ratio. As a reminder, to calculate this ratio you'll need:

1. **Current borrowings** – This is short-term interest-bearing debts, which you'll find on the latest balance sheet under current liabilities.

2. **Non-current borrowings** – Long-term interest-bearing debts listed under non-current liabilities.

3. **Post-tax profits** – Going back five years, although you should have already written these down after calculating profitability. As before I prefer the normalised figure, but you could use the adjusted or reported figures instead.

The steps for calculating the debt ratio are:

1. Calculate the latest total borrowings:

total borrowings = current borrowings + non-current borrowings

2. Calculate five-year average post-tax profit.
3. Calculate the debt ratio as the ratio between total borrowings and five-year average profits:

debt ratio = total borrowings / five-year average post-tax profits

Once I've calculated the debt ratio I then apply one of the following two rules of thumb:

Defensive value rules of thumb

Only invest in a cyclical company if its debt ratio is below 4.

Only invest in a defensive company if its debt ratio is below 5.

These rules of thumb are not drawn out of thin air. The limit of five for defensive companies is based on a rule of thumb that Warren Buffett has apparently used in the past. His rule, according to Mary Buffett in her book *The New Buffettology*, was to look for long-term borrowings to be less than five-times post-tax earnings. The limit of four for cyclical companies is a slightly more cautious version of the same rule and is based on my own hard-won experience.

Calculating the debt ratio is relatively simple so let's run through the process using some of my recent holdings.

BHP Billiton's debt ratio

BHP Billiton is one of the world's largest mining companies and is listed in the FTSE 100. Mining is a cyclical sector and so BHP Billiton needs to have a debt ratio of less than 4 to have what I would consider conservative levels of debt.

To calculate the debt ratio we need the company's normalised profit after tax for the last five years, which is shown in Table 4.2. We'll also need the latest (2014) current and non-current borrowings, which are £2,502m and £17,806m respectively.

Note that BHP Billiton's results are reported in USD (US dollars) and the figures I'm using here have been converted into pounds sterling (the data comes from SharePad).

Year	Post-tax profit (£m)
2010	8,251
2011	14,880
2012	11,330
2013	8,897
2014	8,272

Table 4.2: BHP Billiton profit after tax for five years to 2014

And here's the calculation:

1. Calculate the latest total borrowings:

total borrowings = £2,502m + £17,806 = £20,308m

2. Calculate five-year average post-tax profit:

five-year average post-tax profit = £10,326m

3. Calculate the debt ratio as the ratio between total borrowings and five-year average profits:

debt ratio = £20,308m / £10,326 = 2.0

BHP Billiton's 2014 debt ratio of 2 is well below my maximum of 4 for cyclical companies, so by that measure the company has conservative levels of debt.

Morrisons' debt ratio

As you are probably aware, Wm Morrison Supermarkets is one of the Big Four supermarkets in the UK. It's a member of the FTSE 100 and is listed in the Food & Drug Retailers sector, which is a defensive sector. As a defensive sector company I'm comfortable with it having slightly more debt than a cyclical company, with the cut-off point being a debt ratio of 5.

Table 4.3 shows Morrisons' normalised profit after tax for the five years leading up to its 2015 results. In 2015 it also had current borrowings of £11m and non-current borrowings of £2,508m.

Year	Post-tax profit (£m)
2011	633
2012	650
2013	607
2014	231
2015	220

Table 4.3: Morrisons' post-tax profit for the five years to 2015

The steps to calculate Morrisons' debt ratio are:

1. Calculate the latest total borrowings:

total borrowings = £11m + £2,508m = £2,519m

2. Calculate five-year average post-tax profit

five-year average post-tax profit = £468m

3. Calculate the debt ratio as the ratio between total borrowings and five-year average profits:

debt ratio = £2,519m / £468m = 5.4

With a debt ratio of 5.4, Morrisons is carrying an amount of debt that I would not consider conservative. As a result it's not a company whose shares I would consider buying at the moment. However I do own Morrisons already, having purchased it in 2013, and so this is a good example of how the companies that you invest in will change over time, and not always for the better.

In 2014 and 2015 Morrisons suffered a dramatic decline in profits (which you can see in Table 4.3), largely as a result of the post-financial crisis popularity of discount supermarkets. These weaker results have pulled the company's average profit after tax for the period down from £570m in 2013 to £468m.

Over the same period, total borrowings have gone from £2,432m in 2013 to £2,519m today.

The result of these declining profits and growing debts is that Morrisons' debt ratio has climbed from an acceptable 4.3 in 2013 to an unacceptable 5.4 today. The lesson here is that just because a company has conservative finances today, it does not automatically follow that it will have conservative finances a few years from now. This is why caution at the point of purchase is so important, and even then it does not guarantee a successful outcome.

As for Morrisons, its weaker profits may struggle to cover interest payments along with other fixed expenses, and as the ratio of debt to earnings increases so does the risk that the company will need to raise capital through a rights issue or by selling some of its assets in order to pay down some of those debts.

Although a growing debt ratio isn't enough to make me want to sell Morrisons, it does make it more likely that I'll sell sooner rather than later. Selling is a topic I'll cover in much more detail later on, so that's all I'll say about it for now.

Conservative finances for banks

The core business of a bank is to borrow money from those who have it (by taking in deposits, such as through current accounts) and lend it on to those who need it (in the form of loans and mortgages). Profits come primarily from net interest income, i.e. the difference between the interest income on money it has lent out (say a loan with 6% interest) and the interest expense on money it has borrowed (such as a current account with 3% interest). There's a bit more to it than that of course, but that's the basic picture.

So the entire business of a bank depends on borrowed money. The result is that normal debt ratios (including the one I've just described) are largely useless when analysing banks because they make banks look hopelessly over-leveraged (where leverage means the use of debt as a lever to increase returns).

In my early days as an active investor I simply ignored this problem and assumed that banks, which operate in a highly regulated industry, would always be a safe bet. However, the recent financial crisis blew that theory out of the window and so I spent some time looking for a simple ratio or measure that might separate safer banks from riskier ones. Fortunately banking regulators have come to like the idea of simple ratios and so now I use a ratio which has become a central focus of banks and bank regulators in the wake of the financial crisis.

For that ratio to make sense, I need to briefly outline some of the key ideas that relate to bank balance sheets and how they differ from non-bank balance sheets. This will not be a completely accurate representation of how banks work, but for our purposes it will be more than sufficient.

Bank balance sheets

Imagine a bank that has £100m of customer deposits held across many current accounts. Those are the bank's liabilities (otherwise known as its sources of funds). The bank has loaned £99m of those deposits out to small businesses and homebuyers, leaving £1m in its vault as a daily cash float. Together the loans and the cash make up the bank's assets (otherwise known as its uses of funds).

In that very simple example everything works fine when the loans are all repaid on time, but in the real world some loans are not repaid on time and some are not repaid at all. If £5m of the bank's loans are not repaid (i.e. are defaulted on) the bank would have £100m in liabilities (those current accounts) but only £95m in assets (£94m in loans and £1m in cash). The bank would no longer have enough money to pay back its depositors and so it would be technically insolvent; shareholders would almost certainly be asked to put up additional capital through a rights issue to make the company solvent again.

To avoid this situation, banks have additional sources of funds which can absorb losses more easily than current account deposits. These include some forms of unsecured debt, but the primary buffer in this situation is shareholder equity.

Imagine the same bank as before, but this time instead of having £100m of deposits the bank has £90m. It now also has £10m of capital invested by shareholders, giving it the same £100m of funds as before. If £99m is lent out and if the same £5m of loans is not repaid, it has the same default rate as before, but this time the bank's assets (£94m in loans that will be repaid and £1m cash in the vault) are still worth more than its customers' deposits (£90m). In this scenario those current account holders can still get all their money back and so a rights issue would not be required to raise additional funds.

The difference with the second case is that rather than depositors taking a potential hit, the bank's shareholders have now absorbed the losses. More specifically, shareholder equity has absorbed the losses by declining in value from £10m before those loans were defaulted on to £5m afterwards.

This sounds bad for shareholders, but in reality it may or may not have a material impact on shareholder wealth as the buffer of shareholder equity can be rebuilt in subsequent years, for example if future default rates are below expectations. By having a sufficient buffer of shareholder equity the bank has been able to absorb losses without having to do unpleasant things like suspend dividends or raise additional capital through a rights issue.

The common equity tier 1 ratio

To measure the ratio between a bank's equity buffer and the amount of loans it has made, I use a ratio called the common equity tier 1 ratio (CET1 ratio). Common equity tier 1 is basically shareholder equity with a few adjustments which we don't need to worry about. It is, according to the latest banking regulations, the "highest quality component of a bank's capital".

The CET1 ratio is the ratio between a bank's common equity tier 1 capital and its risk weighted assets (RWA), where RWA is basically the value of the bank's loans and other assets, adjusted upwards or downwards depending on how risky they are deemed to be. In practical terms, the higher the CET1 ratio the more of an equity buffer a bank has against the unexpected.

So looking back at that previous example, with its £10m of shareholder equity and £100m of loans and cash (ignoring the risk weighting of the loans for the sake of simplicity), the CET1 ratio for the bank would be £10m divided by £100m, which is 10%.

One thing I should point out is that while the CET1 ratio is found in the annual and interim results, you will struggle to find it in older results because it's fairly new. However, its predecessor, the core equity tier 1 ratio, is very similar and for our purposes the two are interchangeable. If I refer to CET1 then take that to mean either the common or core equity tier 1 ratio, depending on what was in use at the time.

Table 4.4 shows the CET1 ratio for several leading banks, before the financial crisis and after.

Bank	2007 (pre-crisis)	2013 (post-crisis)
Barclays	7.8%	9.9%
HBOS	7.4%	Taken over by Lloyds in 2009
HSBC	8.1%	12.0%
Lloyds	8.0%	11.0%
Standard Chartered	9.8%	11.8%

Table 4.4: Common equity tier 1 ratios for several leading banks before and after the financial crisis

Before the financial crisis all of the surviving banks in Table 4.4 had lower CET1 ratios than they did a few years after the crisis. It's interesting to see that HBOS, with the lowest pre-crisis ratio, was taken over, while Standard Chartered, with the highest pre-crisis ratio, was barely hurt by the crisis at all (although there were also many other factors, not least of which was the fact that Standard Chartered's business operates primarily in markets that were not hurt so immediately by the crisis).

Of course there is much more to calculating the risks faced by a large bank than simply looking at its CET1 ratio. However, I still think the ratio has a lot of merit to it. It's usually easy to find the number in the annual reports, it's used extensively by the banks themselves and it does appear to have a reasonable correlation to how well each bank withstood the stresses of the financial crisis.

As with many of the financial ratios and metrics in this book, I prefer to look at the average CET1 ratio over a number of years.

Calculating the average CET1 ratio

To calculate the average CET1 ratio you'll need:

1. **Common equity tier 1 ratio (CET1 ratio)** – For the most recent five years. This isn't part of the balance sheet but it should be found fairly prominently towards the beginning of a bank's annual results. Older results may refer to the similar core equity tier 1 ratio instead.

There is only one step to calculating this metric:

1. Calculate the five-year average CET1 ratio

What is a reasonable CET1 ratio?

The latest banking regulations state that a bank must have a CET1 ratio of at least 4.5% at all times. On top of this, an additional buffer of 2.5% (taking the total to 7%) should be built up during good times so that it may, if necessary, be drawn down in bad times. Finally, there is an additional buffer for systemically important banks of up to 2.5%, taking the maximum requirement at any time to 9.5%.

That seems like a fairly reasonable minimum to me. As Table 4.4 shows, before the financial crisis most banks had a CET1 ratio of less than 9.5%. After the crisis they have all moved to ratios above 9.5%.

I want any bank that I invest in to have been slightly more cautious than the maximum caution stipulated by the regulators, so until recently my rule of thumb was to insist that the average of this ratio be 10% at least. However, problems with Standard Chartered (one of my recent holdings) have made me more cautious still and so now my required ratio is even higher (I will talk about improving and evolving the strategy based on your experiences as an investor in Chapter 14).

Defensive value rule of thumb

Only invest in a bank if its five-year average common equity tier 1 ratio is above 12%.

Given that Standard Chartered has had problems, let's calculate its average CET1 ratio to see if it passes the new stricter rule of thumb.

Standard Chartered's common equity tier 1 ratio

Standard Chartered is a FTSE 100-listed bank which operates primarily in Asia, Africa and the Middle East. In recent years it became popular with investors because it came through the financial crisis with barely a scratch on it, largely thanks to its small exposure to Western markets and a relatively strong balance sheet.

Like the combined ratio, the common equity tier 1 ratio doesn't need to be calculated; it will simply be quoted in a bank's annual results. You can see Standard Chartered's CET1 ratios over the last five years in Table 4.5.

Year	CET1 ratio
2010	11.8%
2011	11.8%
2012	11.7%
2013	11.8%

Year	CET1 ratio
2014	10.7%
Average	11.6%

Table 4.5: Standard Chartered CET1 ratio for the five years to 2014

The decline in CET1 from 2013 to 2014 in Table 4.5 was primarily down to regulatory changes, where the ratio being used switched from core equity to common equity, which is calculated in a slightly different way (the common equity ratio is usually slightly lower).

Standard Chartered's average CET1 ratio of 11.6% was, and still is, conservative relative to the ratios maintained at most other major international banks. However, many of those other banks have had enormous problems after the financial crisis and, while Standard Chartered's recent dividend cut and rights issue have been minor in comparison, the fact that they have occurred shows that even a CET1 ratio of more than 10% is not really high enough to be considered conservative.

Standard Chartered's own goal for CET1 beyond 2015 has been increased to the 12% to 13% range, which is why I have increased the CET1 rule of thumb to that level. However, given that new rule of thumb minimum of 12%, Standard Chartered does not make the cut. On that basis I would not describe it as having a history of conservative financing and I would not buy the company's shares at this point in time under my new rules.

Conservative finances for insurance companies

The first thing to note with insurance companies is that, unlike banks, the debt ratio we looked at earlier is still applicable. However, insurance company borrowings must be separated into core structural borrowings and operational borrowings before the ratio can be calculated.

1. **Core structural borrowings** – These form part of the company's capital structure, i.e. part of the capital buffer in the same sense as the common equity buffer that banks use. They are typically unsecured, long-dated borrowings that are less risky than operational borrowings.

2. **Operational borrowings** – These are essentially the same as borrowings in non-financial companies. It is these borrowings which we will use to calculate the debt ratio.

The difference between core structural and operational borrowings will either be obvious from the balance sheet or there will be a note to the accounts which breaks down total borrowings into the two categories, assuming the company makes use of either type of funding.

Since operational borrowings for insurance companies are effectively the same as borrowings for non-financial companies, the debt ratio is calculated in the same way. However, for insurance companies I like to go a step further and look at their capital buffer in much the same way as we did with banks, so let's delve a little deeper into how their balance sheets are structured.

Insurance company balance sheets

Insurance companies exist to spread risk by pooling small, frequent, regular payments from lots of policyholders (known as premiums) in order to cover the costs of large, infrequent, irregular events when they occur (known as claims).

If an insurance company collects more in premiums than it eventually has to pay out in claims and other expenses it will have made a profit on the underwriting side of its business. This is the underwriting profitability we measured with the combined ratio in Chapter 3.

In terms of an insurance company's balance sheet, its main assets are the pool of collected premiums and its main liabilities are the claims it can reasonably expect to have to pay.

As insurance companies have an obligation first and foremost to fulfil their insurance contracts and pay claims promptly, their assets must always exceed their liabilities. The surplus of assets over liabilities is also known as the premium surplus, as it is effectively the surplus of premiums received over expected claim payments. This surplus is very similar to the capital buffer that banks use and it is required for more or less the same reasons.

Here's a quick example:

If an insurance company has £100m of pooled premiums and £99m of expected claims it would have a premium surplus of just £1m. If the value of its pooled premiums decreased by just 2% to £98m then the company would be technically insolvent.

Why would the pool of premiums decrease in value?

The reason is that premiums are often invested to some extent in volatile assets such as equities in order to boost the company's underwriting profit with an additional investment profit. However, as we know, equities can go down as well as up. With a 2% decline in the value of its premium assets, our example insurance company would no longer have enough funds to cover its expected claims. That is not acceptable and so the premium surplus would have to be rebuilt by raising new equity or debt capital, both of which could have a negative impact on shareholder wealth.

This is more or less what happened to many insurance companies such as RSA and Aviva after the dot-com bubble burst. It was a major problem for them and their shareholders.

However, if our example company had £100m in premium assets and £90m of claim liabilities then it would have a premium surplus of £10m. In that case if the premium assets declined in value by 2% to £98m the company would still have a sufficient capital buffer and no additional capital would need to be raised. Shareholders in this company would likely be much better off than in the previous example.

There are lots of different ways to measure an insurance company's capital buffer but I like to use a traditional measure of capital strength known as the premium to surplus ratio.

The premium to surplus ratio

As the name suggests, this is the ratio between premium income (specifically, net written premium) and the premium surplus (usually assumed to be equal to tangible shareholder equity). Here are some definitions:

Net written premium – The amount of premium a company has written during the period in question (typically the financial year) net of reinsurance premiums (where reinsurance is effectively insurance taken out by an insurance company to cover some of the risks it has insured). If, for example, a company wrote a policy for car insurance for £120 per year exactly one month before the end of the financial year, it would still represent £120 of premium written for that year.

In the premium to surplus ratio, net written premium represents the amount of risk an insurance company is taking on, much like the risk weighted assets in a bank's common equity tier 1 ratio.

Tangible shareholder equity – This is simply shareholder equity (total assets minus total liabilities) minus any intangible assets on the balance sheet. This is effectively the capital buffer between an insurance company's expected claims (its liabilities) and its ability to pay those claims (its assets).

However, income statements for insurance companies usually show net earned premium (also known as premium revenue) rather than net written premium, although the difference between premiums earned and written is usually relatively small. This means you'll have to search the annual results looking explicitly for net written premium, although fortunately it is often mentioned towards the start of the document. Generally I would say it is reasonable to calculate the premium to surplus ratio using either net written or net earned premium, but I will assume you're using the more technically correct net written premium.

Here's a quick definition of net earned premium:

Net earned premium – Found on the income statement, but may be referred to as premium revenue. It's the amount of premium an insurance company has earned during the period. Using the previous example of a £120 policy written exactly one month before the year end, the premium earned during the period would be for just that one month, i.e. £10.

Calculating the average premium to surplus ratio

To calculate the five-year average premium to surplus ratio you'll need the following figures covering the last five years:

1. **Net written premium** – This is not always quoted in the income statement so you'll just have to search for it in the annual results (or use net earned premium from the income statement).

2. **Total equity** – On the balance sheet.

3. **Intangible assets** – Listed under non-current assets on the balance sheet.

This is a very simple calculation:

1. Calculate tangible equity for each of the last five years as:

tangible equity = total equity – intangible assets

2. Calculate the premium to surplus ratio for each of the last five years as:

premium to surplus ratio = net written premium / tangible equity

3. Calculate a five-year average for the premium to surplus ratio

What is a prudent premium to surplus ratio?

From both research and experience I have found that a premium to surplus ratio of 2 seems to be a reasonable cut-off point for what could be considered a conservative premium surplus.

Beyond that level insurance companies may be more sensitive to negative shocks and surprises, potentially leading to dividend cuts and/or rights issues. Companies whose ratio is consistently below that limit may be more robust when bad things happen, as they invariably will at some point.

Defensive value rule of thumb

Only invest in an insurance company if its five-year average premium to surplus ratio is less than 2.

Here is a worked example from an insurance company whose shares I have owned quite recently.

RSA Group's premium to surplus ratio

RSA (previously called Royal & Sun Alliance) is a FTSE 100-listed general insurance company, which means it primarily insures things like cars and houses. It has had a pretty rough time of it since the year 2000, with rights issues and dividend cuts on more than one occasion.

Table 4.6 shows how thick its capital buffer has been over the past five years.

Year	Premium (net written premium, £m)	Total equity (£m)	Intangible assets (£m)	Surplus (tangible equity, £m)	Premium to surplus ratio
2010	7,455	3,895	1,209	2,686	2.8
2011	8,138	3,915	1,359	2,556	3.2
2012	8,353	3,879	1,489	2,390	3.5
2013	8,664	3,014	1,103	1,911	4.5
2014	7,465	3,933	800	3,133	2.4
Average					3.3

Table 4.6: RSA Group's average premium to surplus ratio for the five years to 2014

Let's work through the steps to calculate the average premium to surplus ratio:

1. Calculate tangible equity for each of the last five years (here's the 2010 calculation):

2010 tangible equity = £3,895m - £1,209m = £2,686m

2. Calculate the premium to surplus ratio for each of the last five years (again, just for 2010):

2010 premium to surplus ratio = £7,455m / £2,686 = 2.8

3. Calculate a five-year average for the premium to surplus ratio:

five-year average premium to surplus ratio =
(2.8 + 3.2 + 3.5 + 4.5 + 2.4) / 5 = 3.3

RSA's average premium to surplus ratio is 3.3, which is clearly too high for my liking. To make matters worse it is above my preferred maximum of 2 in every single year.

It is perhaps no coincidence that RSA suspended its final dividend for 2013 and launched a £775m rights issue in 2014. If it had maintained a significantly lower premium to surplus ratio then perhaps neither of those undesirable actions would have been required.

Amlin's premium to surplus ratio

Let's have another look at Amlin to see if it has a substantial capital buffer to go along with the high rates of profitability we uncovered earlier. You can see Amlin's average premium to surplus ratio in Table 4.7.

Year	Premium (net written premium, £m)	Total equity (£m)	Intangible assets (£m)	Surplus (tangible equity, £m)	Premium to surplus ratio
2010	1,910	1,730	185	1,545	1.2
2011	2,013	1,420	219	1,202	1.7
2012	2,059	1,498	211	1,286	1.6
2013	2,107	1,679	239	1,440	1.5
2014	2,279	1,786	267	1,519	1.5
Average					1.5

Table 4.7: Amlin's average premium to surplus ratio for the five years to 2014

The premium to surplus ratio for Amlin is below 2 in every single year and therefore – of course – its five-year average is well below 2 as well. Perhaps this is one of the reasons why Amlin was able to maintain its dividend in 2011 even though the company made a substantial loss in that year after several major earthquakes resulted in exceptionally high levels of claims.

As with any financial measure, the premium to surplus ratio is not perfect and a high or low value does not automatically mean an insurance company will or won't run into problems. However, on balance I think it's a useful ratio and quite easy to calculate. It can, in many cases, separate out the riskier insurance companies from the not so risky.

Pension fund liabilities

Another financial obligation that many companies have is a defined benefit pension scheme for their employees. With these schemes the final pension is pre-defined, typically by linking it to an employee's final salary. The company is then legally obliged to pay those pensions, which means that all future pension payments are a financial liability from the company's point of view.

The present value of that liability, i.e. of all future pension payments, can be calculated by actuaries and is recorded at the back of the annual report in the notes to the accounts, where it is usually referred to as *pension liabilities* or *pension obligations*.

To offset that pension liability there will be a pension fund, built up from the savings of employees, which is an asset from the company's point of view. Pension funds contain a collection of income-generating investment assets such as stocks, bonds and property, and it is that income which pays the pensions of retired employees each month.

The difference between a pension scheme's assets and its liabilities is recorded on the balance sheet as either a pension surplus when assets exceed liabilities or as a pension deficit when liabilities exceed assets.

If, for whatever reason, a pension scheme has a large and sustained deficit then the scheme may not be able to afford to pay retirees their pensions. This is obviously not good. In that case the company may have to divert cash from its operations into the pension fund in order to increase the value of the fund's assets and therefore reduce or eliminate the deficit. Of course, any cash which is paid into the pension fund is cash that cannot be invested to grow the business or paid to shareholders as a dividend, so a large pension deficit is something to avoid.

Avoiding large pension fund deficits

In order to avoid large deficits we need to have a working definition of what constitutes a large deficit.

One way to think about this is in terms of the relationship between the deficit and the company's profits. This is an important relationship because if a pension deficit was, for example, ten-times larger than the company's typical profits it would take ten years to reduce that deficit to zero, assuming everything else remained the same.

I don't know about you, but having one of my investments spend ten years funnelling every penny of profit (i.e. it pays no dividends and no capital investments) into its pension fund does not sound like a good idea to me. So having a pension deficit which is ten-times the company's typical profits is very risky indeed.

Such a huge deficit is likely to be very rare, but even much smaller deficits can still be problematic. Based on a mix of research and personal experience, I no longer feel comfortable investing in a company unless it could use its profits to return the pension scheme to a surplus within a single year. On that basis my definition for pension deficits is:

1. **Large pension deficit** – One that is larger than the company's five-year average post-tax profits

2. **Small pension deficit** – One that is smaller than the company's five-year average post-tax profits

The pension fund surplus or deficit is recorded on the balance sheet and so we can easily perform this calculation. But there is a problem with simply measuring the deficit, which I'll explain with another example.

Imagine a company that has average profits of £1m a year, pension assets of £100m and pension liabilities of £99m. The pension scheme has a surplus of £1m (£100m assets minus £99m liabilities), so if we only looked for a deficit we might assume that this company's pension scheme is not a problem because there is no deficit. But what if equity markets, in which the pension fund is partially invested, fell dramatically? Let's assume the pension fund's assets fall in value by 10%, from £100m down to £90m. If that happened the company would find itself with a pension deficit of £9m (£90m assets minus £99m liabilities).

So in a relatively short period of time, quite possibly within one year, the £1m surplus has moved to a £9m deficit. According to my previous definition, the pension scheme has gone from safe (i.e. no deficit) to risky, with a very large deficit (£9m) which is nine-times greater than the company's average profits (£1m).

Hopefully this example shows that a surplus can quickly turn into a deficit and so it is much more important to avoid companies that have large pension liabilities, rather than just those that have large deficits today. If the size of a pension scheme's liabilities is sufficiently small then it will be highly unlikely that the scheme will ever produce a large deficit, no matter what happens to equity, bond or property markets.

Avoiding large pension liabilities

Once again we are in need of a definition, this time for a large pension liability. The key here is to think about how likely it might be for a particular pension scheme to produce a large deficit at some point in the future, rather than whether or not it has one today.

Using the previous example company that has average profits of £1m, if its pension liability was also £1m then it would be near-impossible for the scheme to produce a large deficit. A large deficit for that company would be £1m, but in order to achieve that the pension fund's assets would have become worthless (i.e. the £1m pension liabilities minus worthless assets would give a £1m deficit). That is extraordinarily unlikely short of fraud and nuclear war.

A pension scheme with liabilities that are equal to the company's average profits is probably safe, while one where the liabilities are

100-times the average profits (such as in the original example) is probably very risky.

Where is a reasonable middle ground between those two extremes?

One way to approach this is to work out what sort of deficit we might reasonably expect to see at some point in a pension scheme's future, as a percentage of its liabilities. From that we can then produce a definition for large pension liabilities. This is less complicated than it sounds.

According to the October 2014 Pensions Risk Survey by Mercer, FTSE 350 companies had about £683bn in defined benefit pension liabilities while their pension fund assets totalled £596bn. The total deficit was therefore £87bn, or almost 13% of the value of the liabilities. Given that data, a reasonable assumption is that it's fairly normal, at least in recent years, for a company to have a pension deficit of about 10% of the value of its pension liabilities. In other words, even if a company has a pension surplus today, it is reasonable to expect that the scheme might have a 10% deficit within the next few years, which is within my expected holding period.

From that assumption we can draw up definitions for large and small pension liabilities:

1. **Large pension liability** – One where a typical (10%) deficit would be a large deficit as previously defined.

2. **Small pension liability** – One where a typical (10%) deficit would produce a small deficit as previously defined.

Looking back to the previous example company again, its average earnings are £1m and therefore the definition of a large pension deficit for that company is also £1m. If its pension liabilities were £10m then a typical 10% deficit would have a value of £1m, which means that £10m is the point at which its pension liabilities would be considered large.

In other words, the definitions can be rephrased as:

1. **Large pension liability** – More than ten-times the company's five-year average post-tax profits

2. **Small pension liability** – Less than ten-times the company's five-year average post-tax profits

I call the ratio between a company's pension liabilities and its average profits the **pension ratio**, and it is very similar to the debt ratio we looked at earlier. You may well be able to guess my pension ratio rule of thumb already, but let's work through the calculation anyway.

Calculating the pension ratio

This ratio is almost identical to the debt ratio. You'll need:

1. **Post-tax profits** – Going back five years (which you'll already have by now).

2. **Defined benefit pension scheme liabilities** – You'll find this in the notes to the accounts which are at the back of the full annual report (it's not usually quoted in the preliminary results announcement). It is usually called either pension liabilities or pension obligations.

To calculate the pension ratio, follow these steps:

1. Calculate the average post-tax profit for the last five years.

2. Calculate the pension ratio as:

pension ratio = pension liabilities / five-year average post-tax profits

And here's the rule of thumb associated with this ratio:

Defensive value rule of thumb

Only invest in a company if its pension ratio is less than 10.

In other words, the rule is that a company's pension liabilities are not large, according to the earlier definitions.

Let's look at an example of this ratio in action using another of my recent holdings.

Balfour Beatty's pension ratio

Balfour Beatty is a company which has, at the time of writing, run into some problems. It's a FTSE 250-listed construction company focused on the UK and US markets and in its 2014 annual results management announced that the dividend was being suspended until 2016.

As with any large company that gets into trouble, there are many reasons why Balfour found itself in this position. In my opinion there is at least one cause that was clearly visible if you knew where to look and that is its defined benefit pension scheme.

The company has a large pension fund with a large deficit; so large in fact that Balfour needed to pay almost as much into the fund in the last ten years as it paid out in dividends. Obviously it is not a good idea for so much cash to be flowing out of the company, especially when the payments are like debt interest payments in that the company is obliged to pay them come rain or shine.

Table 4.8 shows just how much cash had to be paid into the pension fund relative to the company's profits and dividends in recent years.

Year	Profit after tax (£m)	Pension deficit payments (£m)	Dividends (£m)
2010	179	81	84
2011	186	113	88
2012	248	61	96
2013	-2	57	96
2014	-310	49	96
Total	301	361	460

Table 4.8: Balfour Beatty's deficit funding payments for the five years to 2014

Here's the calculation for Balfour's pension ratio:

1. Calculate the average post-tax profit for the last five years:

average post-tax profit =
(£179m + £186m + £248m – £2m – £310m) / 5 = £60.2m

2. Calculate the pension ratio for 2014 (in 2014 the company had defined benefit pension obligations of £3,518m):

2014 pension ratio = £3,518m / £60.2m = 58.4

Clearly Balfour Beatty's pension ratio is way above my rule of thumb maximum of 10. You could argue that the company has made losses in recent years, which have reduced its average profits, and that the average profits figure should in fact be considerably higher to reflect the true earnings potential of the company.

However, even if we were incredibly generous and said that Balfour's average profits were in fact equal to the highest profits the company had made in the last five years, i.e. £248m, its pension ratio would still be above 14 and still above my preferred maximum.

In my opinion Balfour Beatty has a pension fund which is far too large for the company, to the point where the primary function of the company today is to feed cash into the pension fund to reduce its deficit.

Combining the debt ratio and pension ratio

One final check, which I've recently added to my conservative financing checklist, is to put a limit on how much interest-bearing debt and pension liabilities a company can have in total.

The idea is simple: if a defensive sector company has a debt ratio of 4.8 then its debts are acceptable according to the debt ratio rule of thumb, but only just. If that same company also has a pension ratio of 9.2 then that is also acceptable, but again, only just. Both of these relatively high ratios represent risks to the business, but they are not independent risks. If a company has to pay out a large portion of its profits as debt interest payments then it will be far less able to pay off a large pension deficit at the same time, and vice versa.

So a defensive company with a debt ratio of 4.8 may – just about – be carrying an acceptable amount of debt, but that won't be true if it also has a large pension scheme.

To avoid the risks that come from a combination of large debts and large pension liabilities, I have one final rule of thumb for conservative finances.

Defensive value rule of thumb

Only invest in a company if its combined debt and pension ratio is below 10.

To combine the debt and pension ratios I just add them together. So, for example, a company with a debt ratio of 3 and a pension ratio of 5 would be okay according to this rule, while a company with a debt ratio of 4 and a pension ratio of 8 would not.

In the next chapter we'll compare a company's share price to its past earnings and dividends as we begin to think about whether or not the shares are good value for money.

But first, here is a summary of the rules of thumb covered in this chapter.

Rules of thumb for conservative finances

- Only invest in a cyclical company if its debt ratio is below 4.

- Only invest in a defensive company if its debt ratio is below 5.

- Only invest in a bank if its five-year average common equity tier 1 ratio is above 12%.

- Only invest in an insurance company if its five-year average premium to surplus ratio is less than 2.

- Only invest in a company if its pension ratio is less than 10.

- Only invest in a company if its combined debt and pension ratio is below 10.

CHAPTER 5.

Low Valuation

"The price paid for each [company] should be reasonable in relation to its average earnings for the last five years or longer."

BENJAMIN GRAHAM

Using the tools we've looked at so far, relatively defensive companies should be easy to find. Just pick a company, check for a ten-year unbroken dividend record and calculate its growth rate, growth quality, profitability and so on. If it has consistent inflation-beating growth, powered by high levels of profitability and little debt, it could be worth investing in.

However, I have said nothing about price or value, and the title of this book is *The Defensive Value Investor*, not *The Defensive Investor*.

It's no good finding a fantastically defensive company if it currently trades on a PE of 50 and has a dividend yield of 1%. In that case even if the company quadrupled in size over the next decade the share price might not go anywhere.

How does this work? How can corporate growth not result in a rising share price?

Imagine a company that investors thought was about to grow quickly. In that case they might accept a smaller earnings yield and dividend yield today, so they're willing to accept the PE of 50 and dividend yield of 1% mentioned before. Let's assume the company's share price is 100p while earnings are 2p and the dividend is 1p.

After ten years the company has done exactly as investors expected. Its earnings have grown to 8p and the dividend is up to 4p, so its financial results have quadrupled in a decade, which requires a growth rate of about 15% a year. However, the company's growth spurt is over and investors now expect growth in line with inflation, perhaps 2% a year or thereabouts.

With such paltry future growth investors may now only be willing to give the company a PE ratio of 12.5 and a dividend yield of 4%, both of which are fairly normal values for slower growth companies. Surprisingly enough, with those valuation metrics the share's price would still be 100p; unchanged from its level a decade before, despite the underlying company growing at 15% a year.

The lesson from this example is hopefully clear: the price you pay for a company is every bit as important as the company's growth rate.

In this chapter I'll work through how I think about price and value and in particular a couple of twists I apply to the standard PE ratio and dividend yield.

Problems with the PE ratio

When it comes to valuing companies, investors generally stick to using simple valuation ratios. The most common is the price to earnings (PE) ratio mentioned above, which compares the current share price to last year's earnings per share.

The price to earnings ratio is calculated as follows:

PE = share price / earnings per share

Value investors will often look for low PE ratios and at first glance that makes a lot of sense. A low PE ratio means a high earnings yield and that means more earnings for each pound invested. Since earnings are the starting point for dividends, and are the source of much internal investment within companies, getting a higher earnings return on your investment is generally a good thing.

However, there are several problems with the standard PE ratio, the biggest of which is its focus on a single year's earnings.

The problem here is that earnings can go up or down dramatically and unpredictably from one year to the next, even for quite defensive companies. For example, the earnings of Aviva, the insurance giant, went from 45.4p in 2004 to 86.6p in 2006 for a 91% gain in two years, but by 2007 they had dropped back again by 44%.

Does that mean Aviva was worth 44% less in 2007 than it was in 2006? I don't think it does. I don't think a property investor would say a house had halved in value just because rental income had halved in a single year (perhaps because of a problem tenant). A sensible investor would say that one year was a blip and that the true ability of the house to produce an income was more or less unchanged.

As an equity investor I want to think about companies in much the same way that property investors think about property. I want to ignore short-term ups and downs and instead think about the long-term value of a company rather than its earnings over a single 12-month period.

A PE ratio for long-term investors

The solution is simple. Instead of comparing price to last year's earnings, it is better to compare a company's share price to its average earnings over a number of years. That's because a company's average earnings over the previous ten years (known as a ten-year moving average) will change much less from one year to the next than a single year's earnings.

For example, a company's 2015 earnings could easily be double or half its 2014 earnings. However, if the company has been profitable in every year for the past ten years then its average earnings from 2004-2014 are unlikely to be very different to its average earnings over the 2005-2015 period. The stability of long-term average earnings gives us something significantly more robust to compare share prices against than a company's most recent one-year earnings.

It was Professor Robert Shiller of Yale University who popularised the idea of comparing current prices to long-term average earnings, although the concept dates back at least to Benjamin Graham, who originally wrote about it in the 1930s.

Shiller's approach is to use the ten-year inflation adjusted earnings average in a ratio which is now known as the cyclically adjusted PE (CAPE). By applying CAPE to the S&P 500 index (the US large-cap index), Shiller was able to show that the US market in the year 2000 was clearly expensive and likely to fall back towards historically normal valuation levels. At the time many investors were caught up in the dot-com mania and thought the market would just keep going up and up.

The decade of subsequent poor returns from that index (and the FTSE 100 as well, which was similarly overvalued) are strong proof that Shiller and his valuation tool were right. In other words, CAPE gave investors a broadly correct indication of long-term returns, which is something the standard PE ratio rarely manages to do.

Figure 5.1 shows the difference in volatility between real (inflation adjusted) annual earnings and cyclically-adjusted earnings (i.e. the ten-year average) for the S&P 500 index. I'm using that index rather than the FTSE 100 because its earnings data goes back over 100 years, which will help to show these volatility differences much more clearly.

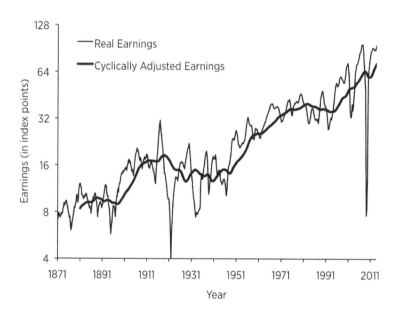

Figure 5.1: S&P 500 earnings volatility over more than a century

Measured on an annual basis, earnings move around a lot. On the other hand, cyclically-adjusted earnings are far more stable, reflecting the relatively stable earnings power of the 500 largest companies in the US economy. This gives us a much steadier number to compare price against, and that applies whether we're talking about the S&P 500, the FTSE 100 or even a single company (although this approach is most suited to relatively defensive companies).

Valuation mean reversion

The next valuable insight from CAPE is that it is a mean reverting ratio, which means it tends to head back towards its long-term average figure given enough time. Occasionally it will wander off to extreme highs (like 1999) or extreme lows (like 2009), but for the most part CAPE stays fairly close to its long-term average.

Figure 5.2 shows this mean reverting tendency for the S&P 500.

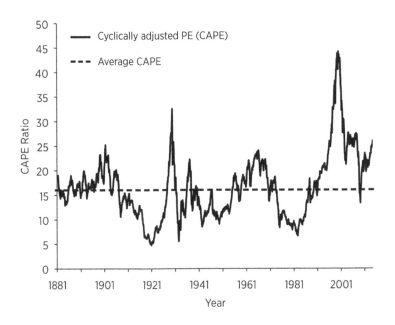

Figure 5.2: Mean reversion of the S&P 500 CAPE ratio

The index's CAPE valuation has repeatedly swung back and forth, from above to below its long-run average, for more than a century. This tendency to mean revert is caused, at least in part, by what is known as the replacement cost of businesses.

As share prices increase it eventually becomes much cheaper to own a company (perhaps a widget manufacturer) by creating a new one from scratch than it is to buy an existing one through the stock market. This increases the supply of new companies and reduces the number of stock market buyers, both of which tend to lower share prices. The result is an effective limit to how high share prices can go.

The same principle applies when shares are very cheap. At some point it will make more sense to buy an existing company cheaply on the stock market than to start one up from scratch. This decreases the supply of new companies and increases the number of stock market buyers, both of which tend to raise share prices. The result is an effective limit to how low share prices can go.

In between those two extremes the market will bounce around randomly, driven by news and the opinions and emotions of investors.

Figure 5.2 shows that for the most part, investors are happy to buy and sell when CAPE is somewhere between 10 and 20. When the market moves well away from that range it eventually falls back towards its average value of about 16. It may take a few years to do it, but if history is anything to go by the odds are that this mean reversion will continue long into the future.

Mean reversion is an important idea because it suggests that if you buy an index when its price is well below its long-term average CAPE ratio, the ratio is more likely to move upwards and back towards its long-term average over the next few years.

Since the ten-year average earnings figure is relatively stable this increase in the CAPE ratio is more likely to come from a rising price than a decline in average earnings. If this occurs the upward movement in price will give a boost to shareholder returns (not to mention the higher yields which are also typically available at lower CAPE ratios). In other words, valuation mean reversion is the engine that drives the buy low and sell high tactic, which is at the core of any value investment strategy.

Although CAPE and the notion of comparing price to long-term average earnings is usually only applied to market indices such as the S&P 500 and FTSE 100, I think these ideas can just as effectively be applied to relatively defensive individual companies.

Calculating a long-term PE ratio

While CAPE is based on inflation-adjusted earnings, I think that virtually the same benefits can be achieved without adjusting earnings for inflation, which makes the ratio that bit easier to calculate.

The non-inflation-adjusted version of CAPE is usually known as PE10 and it is calculated as follows:

1. Calculate the ten-year average EPS

2. Calculate the PE10 ratio as:

PE10 = current share price / ten-year average EPS

My rule of thumb for PE10 has as its starting point a quote from Benjamin Graham:

> "We would not recommend a price exceeding twenty times [the company's five-year average] earnings. This would protect the investor against the common problem of buying good stocks at high levels of the general market. It would also bar the purchase, even in normal markets, of

a number of fine issues which sell at unduly high prices in anticipation of greatly increased future earnings."

For our purposes Graham's formula of 20 times the five-year earnings average needs a slight tweak. I use the ten-year earnings average, which for growing companies will typically be lower than the five-year average, and more so if the company is growing quickly. There is no magic correct number, but I have found that companies trading at more than 30 times their ten-year average earnings are unlikely to fit the description of a value investment.

On that basis I have the following rule of thumb:

Defensive value rule of thumb

Only invest in a company if its PE10 ratio is below 30.

I'll calculate this PE10 ratio for a couple of real-world examples in a moment, but first I want to show you how these ideas about cyclically-adjusted earnings can be applied to dividends as well.

A dividend ratio for long-term investors

Much of our analysis into the quality and defensiveness of a company has been based on its dividend track record, where we have primarily focused on how consistently and quickly the company had been able to increase its dividend payments to shareholders.

While the consistency and speed of dividend growth are clearly important to an investment's total return, just as important is the dividend yield. The dividend yield can be measured using historic dividends or a forecast of future dividends. I prefer to use historic dividends so here's my definition of the (historic) dividend yield:

dividend yield = last year's total dividend / current share price

This is the dividend yield that you'll see quoted on almost every investment website. It's also available from just about every data provider, including the ones listed in the appendix.

However, the dividend yield suffers from many of the same problems as the PE ratio. Perhaps not to the same extent as dividends tend to be more stable than earnings from one year to the next, but the basic problems that come from focusing on a single year's results are still there.

As with earnings, if a company's dividend is cut by 50%, does that mean the whole company is worth 50% less than before? Perhaps in some cases it does, but for high quality and relatively defensive companies I think in most cases it does not. A more likely story is that the company has hit some sort of short or medium-term problem that requires a dividend cut in order to rectify it. In my experience the dividend will often recover, although it may take several years.

That's not to say I don't look at the dividend yield, because I do, but it is not my primary dividend ratio.

I think a better way to find shares that are cheap relative to their past dividends is to use the dividend equivalent of the PE10 ratio, i.e. the PD10 ratio. This is exactly what it sounds like; it's the ratio between a company's current share price and its long-term (ten-year) average dividend. It provides a much more stable ratio than the standard dividend yield.

Calculating a long-term dividend ratio

To calculate the PD10 ratio you'll need the company's per share dividend payments (DPS) for the last ten years. The steps are:

1. Calculate the ten-year average DPS

2. Calculate the PD10 ratio as:

PD10 = current share price / ten-year average DPS

My rule of thumb for this ratio is shown below.

Defensive value rule of thumb

Only invest in a company if its PD10 ratio is below 60.

This maximum value of 60 comes from combining the PE10 maximum of 30 with the idea that a reasonable long-term level of dividend cover for most companies is two (dividend cover is the ratio between earnings and dividends per share and is calculated as EPS divided by DPS). So a company where earnings consistently covered the dividend twice over (i.e the dividend cover was two), and whose share price resulted in a PE10 ratio of 30, would also have a PD10 ratio of 60.

As with the PE10 maximum of 30, there is nothing magical about the PD10 maximum of 60 which says that shares below that level are cheap and those above it are expensive. However, shares trading beyond that sort of level are far less likely to be cheap and are more likely to be either expensive or relying on rapid future growth to justify the current price, and I am not interested in investing in either of those situations.

Stocks with PD10 ratios above 60 are also more likely to have below average dividend yields as well, which will be of interest to more income-focused investors.

Let's take a look at some examples.

BAE Systems' valuation ratios

These valuation ratios are simple to calculate, so applying them to a real company will only take a few moments. In this case I'll apply them to BAE Systems, a FTSE 100 company that operates in the Aerospace & Defence sector. It is the UK's largest manufacturing company. As at the 2014 results, BAE had a growth rate of 6.4% and growth quality of 81%, both of which are above average.

You can see BAE's earnings and dividend per share over the last ten years in Table 5.1.

Year	Normalised earnings per share (p)	Dividend per share (p)
2005	15.3	10.3
2006	16.3	11.3
2007	30.2	12.8
2008	51.1	14.5
2009	30.4	16.0
2010	40.4	17.5
2011	43.5	18.8
2012	28.1	19.5

Year	Normalised earnings per share (p)	Dividend per share (p)
2013	32.5	20.1
2014	38.0	20.5
Average	32.6	16.1

Table 5.1: BAE Systems' results to 2014

In addition to earnings and dividends per share for the last ten years, we also need the share price. For this example I'll use the price as it was in May 2015, which was 509p.

We can calculate BAE Systems' PE10 ratio using the previously described steps:

1. Calculate the ten-year average EPS:

ten-year average EPS =
(15.3 + 16.3 + 30.2 + 51.1 + 30.4 + 40.4 + 43.5 + 28.1 + 32.5 + 38.0) / 10 = 32.6p

2. Calculate the PE10 ratio:

PE10 = 509p / 32.6p = 15.6

Calculating PD10 is more or less the same:

3. Calculate the ten-year average DPS:

ten-year average DPS =
(10.3 + 11.3 + 12.8 + 14.5 + 16.0 + 17.5 + 18.8 + 19.5 + 20.1 + 20.5) / 10 = 16.1p

4. Calculate the PD10 ratio:

PD10 = 509p / 16.1p = 31.6

Both BAE's PE10 ratio and PD10 ratio are comfortably below my rule of thumb maximums of 30 and 60 respectively, so according to those rules BAE wasn't obviously overvalued at 509p.

ARM Holdings' valuation ratios

ARM Holdings is a FTSE 100-listed technology company that develops and licences technologies which are included in many modern gadgets such as smartphones and tablets. As at the 2014 results the company had a growth rate of 23.1% and growth quality of 89%, both of which are among the highest of any company in the FTSE All-Share.

You can see the company's earnings and dividend per share over the last ten years in Table 5.2.

Year	Normalised earnings per share (p)	Dividend per share (p)
2005	2.1	0.5
2006	3.0	1
2007	2.7	2
2008	3.5	2.2
2009	3.8	2.4
2010	6.4	2.9
2011	8.2	3.5
2012	11.7	4.5

Year	Normalised earnings per share (p)	Dividend per share (p)
2013	11.1	5.7
2014	18.1	7.0
Average	7.1	3.2

Table 5.2: ARM Holdings' results to 2014

Once again we need the share price and for ARM Holdings I'll use the price as it was in August 2015, which was 865p.

We can calculate ARM Holdings' PE10 ratio using the same steps as before:

1. Calculate the ten-year average EPS:

ten-year average EPS =
(2.1 + 3.0 + 2.7 + 3.5 + 3.8 + 6.4 + 8.2 + 11.7 + 11.1 + 18.1) / 10 = 7.1p

2. Calculate the PE10 ratio:

PE10 = 865p / 7.1p = 121.8

Calculate PD10:

3. Calculate the ten-year average DPS:

ten-year average DPS =
(0.5 + 1.0 + 2.0 + 2.2 + 2.4 + 2.9 + 3.5 + 4.5 + 5.7 + 7.0) / 10 = 3.2p

4. Calculate the PD10 ratio:

PD10 = 865p / 3.2p = 270.3

ARM Holdings was clearly trading way outside my rule of thumb maximums, indicating that the shares were not obviously cheap.

But saying the shares were not obviously cheap is not the same as saying they are expensive. If the company continued to grow at 20% plus per year for many years (as it had done in the past) then it may eventually justify those lofty valuation ratios. However, relying on rapid future growth to justify a company's current share price is the province of growth investors, not defensive value investors.

This means that as things stand today, I would probably not consider investing in ARM unless its share price dropped to around 200p, which seems unlikely at the moment.

In the next chapter we will look at several ways to combine the various *defensive factors* such as growth rate and growth quality, with the *value factors* of PE10 and PD10, in order to find shares that have a good balance of both defensiveness and value.

But first, here are those valuation rules of thumb once again.

Rules of thumb for low valuations

- Only invest in a company if its PE10 ratio is below 30.

- Only invest in a company if its PD10 ratio is below 60.

CHAPTER 6.

Defensiveness and Value Combined

"What we're trying to get at is buying above-average companies, high return on capital companies but only when they're available at below-average prices."

PROFESSOR JOEL GREENBLATT

Now that we have a range of defensive factors and valuation factors we can use them to quickly narrow down the list of companies we might be interested in.

This narrowing down of potential investment candidates is an important step because calculating a company's defensive value factors typically takes just a few minutes (especially when using a spreadsheet), while the more detailed business analysis in Part 2 can take several hours. So the rational thing to do first is quickly review a company using the defensive value factors and then only carry out a more detailed business review if its growth rate, profitability and so on look sufficiently attractive.

There are many different ways that these factors can be used to select stocks, so I'll outline several of them in this chapter, although only one of them is the method I actually use.

Method 1: Using the rules of thumb

As an absolute minimum I would say that any investment candidate should, at the very least, pass all of the various rules of thumb. Once you've calculated all the factors the stock should, for example, have:

1. Paid a dividend in every one of the last ten years

2. A ten-year dividend cover of more than 1

3. Growth quality of more than 50%

4. A growth rate of more than 2%

5. Profitability of more than 7%

This list should continue and include all of the relevant debt ratios and valuation ratios as well.

The problem with this approach is that these rules of thumb represent a set of bare minimum standards, primarily put in place to avoid basket-case companies or clearly overvalued companies. They certainly do not define defensive companies or good value shares.

I use this method as a minimum to help me avoid stocks that do not meet all of the rules of thumb, but I then move on to apply much more strict criteria as well.

Method 2: Using stricter pre-defined criteria

Perhaps the obvious way to use the defensive value factors is to define your own criteria and then only perform a detailed business analysis on (and perhaps eventually purchase) shares that meet those criteria. Although I don't use this method myself I'll give you a couple of examples in case this ends up being your preferred approach.

Example 1: Focusing on defensiveness and quality

Everybody has slightly different ideas about what a good investment is, and that is as true of defensive value investors as anybody else. Perhaps you have a preference for higher growth, extremely consistent and profitable companies, and you are willing to accept a slightly higher valuation and lower dividend yield in order to buy them (generally higher quality, higher growth companies trade on higher valuations).

In that case your criteria will still be at least as strict as my rules of thumb across all the various factors and metrics, but in some specific ways your rules would be far stricter.

You might, for example, insist on some of the following:

1. Growth rate of at least 10% (rather than 2%)

2. Growth quality of at least 85% (rather than 50%)

3. Profitability of at least 15% (rather than 7%)

4. Debt ratio of less than 3 (rather than 4 or 5)

For the valuation factors you might simply use the existing rules of thumb, i.e. PE10 ratio below 30 and PD10 ratio below 60. You may not even care if the dividend yield is below the market average. While this would not represent a cheap share to most value investors, it could still be excellent value if the company is of exceptional quality, as implied by its high and consistent growth and profitability, and relatively light use of debt.

Example 2: Focusing on yield and value

Not everybody is obsessed with high growth, high quality companies. Some people want a good dividend yield today, and in order to get it you typically have to invest in slower growth companies. But that's okay, and high yield investing is an entirely acceptable approach for many investors.

If a high dividend yield was your main goal then you might use criteria for the defensive value factors such as:

1. PE10 ratio of less than 20 (rather than 30)

2. PD10 ratio of less than 40 (rather than 60)

3. Dividend yield of at least 4% (rather than no rule at all)

4. Growth rate of at least 5% (rather than 2%)

5. Growth quality of at least 75% (rather than 50%)

Again, you might decide that for other factors, such as profitability or the debt ratio, the default rule of thumb maximums and minimums would be fine.

You might even decide to use multiple criteria for stocks in your portfolio. You could use criteria similar to both of the previous examples and fill a portfolio with a mix of defensive-growth stocks and defensive-income stocks. The choices are endless.

As for rules of thumb for this method, I don't have any because this isn't the method I use to make initial stock selections. However, a reasonable approach might be to insist that a stock meet all or at least most of your chosen criteria.

Since this isn't how I select stocks for further analysis, let's move on and look at another alternative. This next method is much closer to how I think about and perform stock selection.

Method 3: Comparing stocks against the market average

As an active investor I'm fairly sure that one of your goals is, at least in some way, to outperform the market. After all, we can easily get the market return by simply buying and holding a low-cost index tracker.

In my case I want my portfolio to beat the UK market (which I class as either the FTSE 100 or FTSE All-Share, since they are virtually the same in terms of performance) in the following ways:

1. **Higher yield** – Have a higher dividend yield than the market at all times

2. **Higher growth** – Produce higher dividend and capital growth than the market over the medium term

3. **Lower risk** – Be less volatile and show smaller declines than the market over the medium term

For the sake of simplicity I'll assume that your goals are similar. One way to achieve those goals is to invest in a diverse group of stocks that have – on average – higher yields than the market, higher growth rates than the market and lower valuation ratios than the market. Low valuations are important in this context because, thanks to valuation mean reversion, lower valuation ratios make it more likely that a company's share price will increase rather than decline, or at least decline by less than the market.

We can find out whether a given stocks fits that description, or at least comes close to it, by comparing its defensive value factors directly against the market's defensive value factors. In other words, we can calculate the growth rate, growth quality and so on for the market index and then compare a given stock directly to that.

Let's get the ball rolling by calculating the defensive value factors for the UK market.

The FTSE 100's defensive value factors

To compare a stock to the FTSE 100 we need the index's current price and its revenues, earnings and dividends for the last ten years. Unfortunately earnings and dividend payments for the FTSE 100 are not the easiest things to find, but we can get around that by calculating those figures from the index's price, its PE ratio and its dividend yield. I'll work through the calculation first and then explain a bit more about where you can find the data.

You can calculate the FTSE 100's earnings and dividends at a particular point in time in the following way:

FTSE 100 earnings = FTSE 100 price / FTSE 100 PE

FTSE 100 dividends = FTSE 100 price × FTSE 100 dividend yield

Note that the earnings and dividend values produced are in index points rather than pounds, but that is in fact preferable for our purposes.

Revenue figures for the FTSE 100 are, in my experience, simply impossible to find. However, an easy workaround is to take the dividend value and multiply it by 10 (the exact multiple doesn't really matter) to get a rough ballpark estimate of revenues:

FTSE 100 revenues estimate = FTSE 100 dividends × 10

I base this revenues estimate on dividends because revenues are generally quite stable from year to year and in that respect they are somewhat similar to dividends. Given that the revenues estimate has to be based on something, I think basing it on dividends is reasonable. This estimate will of course be wrong, but it's good enough for our purposes and enables us to calculate the index's growth rate and growth quality.

To save you the bother of having to find all the underlying data and do all the calculations, I've taken the FTSE 100's price, PE ratio and dividend yield at the end of each of the last ten years and calculated the corresponding revenues, earnings and dividends values. You can find a table containing that data and another containing the index's latest defensive value factors in the appendix. All you need to do is recalculate the PE10 and PD10 ratios for the index based on its current price.

You'll also need to calculate the FTSE 100's revenue, earnings and dividend data for 2016 and beyond as time goes by. To calculate the figures for a given year I take the index's price, PE ratio and dividend yield as at the last day of the year and then use the previous calculations.

I prefer to get this data from the *Financial Times* (FT) website, which has a handy archive of index data going back several years. You can find a link to the FT data archive in the appendix.

This approach of selecting stocks based on how they compare against the market average will make a lot more sense when we work through an example.

Comparing Vodafone to the market

Vodafone is, as I'm sure you are aware, a FTSE 100-listed company which operates in the Mobile Telecoms sector. Table 6.1 shows the defensive value factors for Vodafone and the FTSE 100 as they were at the beginning of May 2015 (with the FTSE 100's factors based on its revenues, earnings and dividends as at the end of 2014).

May 2015	Vodafone	FTSE 100
Price	231p	6961
Growth rate	6.1%	2.0%
Growth quality	92.6%	59.3%
Profitability	7.4%	10.0% (estimated)
PE10	13.2	14.8
PD10	26.4	34.5
Number of wins	2 defensive and 2 value wins	1 defensive and 0 value wins

Table 6.1: Comparison of Vodafone and the FTSE 100 in May 2015

According to Table 6.1, Vodafone was an acceptable investment candidate because it passed all of the basic rules of thumb that we have looked at so far. On top of that it clearly offered a better combination of defensiveness and value in May 2015 than the FTSE 100. The company's growth rate and growth quality were both better than the market's and its shares could be bought on lower PE10 and PD10 ratios. Income-focused investors might also have been pleased to know that Vodafone had a higher dividend yield of 4.8% compared to the FTSE 100's yield of 3.3%.

The only factor where Vodafone didn't win against the market was profitability, where its relatively low result of 7.4% was only just above my 7% rule of thumb minimum. As you can see I've used an estimated value for the market's profitability, and that's because the data for calculating the true value is not available. However, an estimate of 10% is close to the average profitability of the 230 or so stocks that I keep track of, and it's a nice round number which is easy to remember.

One possible rule of thumb for this approach would be to insist that stocks beat the market on most of these five key factors, in other words on at least three out of five, as Vodafone has done here. If you're an income-focused investor then you might also insist that any stock beat the market's dividend yield as well. According to that rule of thumb, in May 2015 Vodafone was a good candidate for further analysis because it beat the market on four out of the five key factors.

Of course, just because Vodafone beat the market across most of those factors at that particular point in time, it does not automatically follow that the shares would outperform the market going forward. However, since the assumed goal here is to beat the market I think that selecting stocks with many market-beating factors is a very sensible place to start.

Let's run through another example before moving on to the fourth and final stock selection method.

Comparing SABMiller to the market

For this second example I've chosen SABMiller, one of the world's largest beverage companies. This time the comparison uses the company's share price and the FTSE 100's price in August 2015. You can see how the two investments stack up in Table 6.2.

August 2015	SABMiller	FTSE 100
Price	3365p	6693
Growth rate	11.4%	2.0%
Growth quality	81.5%	59.3%
Profitability	7.4%	10.0% (estimated)
PE10	32.9	14.2

August 2015	SABMiller	FTSE 100
PD10	73.4	33.2
Number of wins	2 defensive and 0 value wins	1 defensive and 2 value wins

Table 6.2: Comparison of SABMiller and the FTSE 100 in August 2015

This comparison gives us some idea of where SABMiller sits on the defensive/value continuum. It is clearly not a traditional value investment as its PE10 and PD10 ratios are both above my rule of thumb maximums of 30 and 60 respectively. However, in a situation like this you may still want to know how the company compares to the market in order to see whether or not it could be an attractive investment at a lower price. So let's continue the analysis with that in mind.

Like Vodafone, SABMiller wins on two of the three defensive factors, with a higher growth rate and growth quality than the market. However, it fails to win on any of the value factors and so only beats the market on two out of the five factors. Income investors might also have noted that SABMiller's dividend yield was 2.1% at the time compared to a yield of 3.5% for the FTSE 100.

So in August 2015 it looked like SABMiller might be an acceptably defensive company, given that its growth rate and growth quality were both better than the market average. However, it was primarily the value factors, driven by the company's share price, which were holding back its attractiveness.

But share prices can change quite rapidly. If SABMiller's share price were to fall far enough its value factors could improve to the point where it might be worthy of further analysis and even investment. The good news is that we can calculate a target purchase price fairly easily and then do a deep analysis of the business only if that target level is reached.

The process for calculating a target purchase price is the same for any of methods 1, 2 or 3, so let's have a look at how that works in practice.

Calculating a target purchase price for methods 1, 2 and 3

If you use any of methods 1, 2 or 3 to select stocks for further analysis, you're likely to run into this problem of attractive companies trading at unattractive prices. These three methods are essentially the same in that they compare a stock's current valuation ratios against some predefined limit (either a value set by you or the values from the FTSE 100). Since we know the maximum value that we would like those ratios to be under, it's a simple process to calculate the share price that would give us the PE10 and PD10 ratios we're after.

Let's use SABMiller as the example again. The problem in August 2015 was its share price and valuation ratios. They were, quite simply, too high for the company to be considered a defensive value investment when compared against either the default rules of thumb or the FTSE 100.

Given that SABMiller only beat the FTSE 100 on two out of the five factors, it would need at least one of its valuation ratios to fall below those of the FTSE 100 in order for it to be considered attractively priced (using the previous guideline of attractively priced stocks having to beat the market on three or more factors). This means its PE10 ratio would need to fall below 14.2 or its PD10 ratio would need to fall below 33.2.

We can calculate the share price required to hit each of these targets quite easily. Let's start with the PE10 target. Note that while the figures I use here are in pence, SABMiller publishes its results in US dollars. Conversion from dollars to pounds is a useful feature of many data providers, and in this case I'm using data from SharePad.

SABMiller had ten-year average earnings of 102.3p. To achieve a PE10 ratio of 14.2 it would need a share price of no more than 14.2 times its ten-year average earnings, i.e.:

target share price = 10-yr average earnings × required PE10

Plugging in the numbers for this example gives:

target share price = 102.3p × 14.2 = 1,453p

So the target share price, based on achieving the required PE10 ratio, would be 1,453p. Given that the share price at the time was 3,365p that would require a drop in the price of 56.8%. That seems somewhat unlikely, so let's turn to calculating a target price using PD10.

The company had a ten-year average dividend of 45.8p. To achieve a market-beating PD10 ratio of 33.2 or less, SABMiller would need a share price no more than 33.2 times its ten-year average dividend, i.e.:

target share price = 10-yr average dividend x required PD10

Plugging in the numbers again gives:

target share price = 45.8p × 33.2 = 1,521p

The target share price of 1,521p is slightly more achievable than the PE10-based target, but only just.

In this case SABMiller only needs one additional factor to beat the market for it to be a potentially interesting investment, so 1,521p would be the target price.

If both valuation ratios needed to beat the market (if, for example, the company only beat the market on one of the three defensive factors) then you would need to pick the lower of the two price targets.

Obviously 1,521p is a long way below 3,365p and in all likelihood SABMiller's shares will never get that low again. But you never know. It really isn't that unusual for large-cap stocks to fall by 50% or more if they run into significant (but preferably not life-threatening) problems, and it takes next to no effort to calculate a target price and then add a company's shares to a watch list.

A watch list can be a paper list that you look at each week or month, or you can use a spreadsheet or online tool. Either way, I think a watch list of potential investments and target purchase prices is one of the most useful things an investor can have.

With the three stock selection methods we've looked at so far, while there are some differences, they can all be applied through the following fairly flexible rule of thumb.

Defensive value rule of thumb

Only invest in a company if it meets a sufficient number of your pre-defined criteria.

In the previous examples I have used three out of five as a sufficient number, but you may want your stocks to pass four or even five of your criteria. However, the stricter your requirements the more difficult it will be to find suitable investments, so there is a balance to be struck.

As I have said though, I don't use any of these methods to do my initial stock selection. The one I use is similar to method 3 in that both are based on the idea of searching for stocks that have market-beating attributes, but the details are different. So let's turn, at last, to the initial stock selection method which I actually use on a day-to-day basis.

Method 4: Calculating a defensive value rank

Methods 1, 2 and 3 all share one main advantage: they are easy to use. If you want an easy system for selecting companies for further analysis then those may be the ones to go for.

However, their simplicity is also a weakness. If two stocks both meet the various pre-defined criteria (whether defined by you or the market average) then those approaches will consider the stocks equally attractive. But what if one of the companies is growing twice as quickly as the other? What if the PE10 ratio of one is half that of the other? You could use judgment to discern between them, but in such cases methods 1, 2 and 3 have nothing to say, even though it's fairly obvious that one stock is likely to be a better choice than the other, all else being equal.

One way to take account of these differences in a systematic way is to use a ranking system, which is only really viable when a spreadsheet does most of the work. The ranking method is one I first came across in *The Little Book that Beats the Market* by Professor Joel Greenblatt.

The basic idea is to rank investments based on each of their defensive value factors in turn, and then combine those separate ranks into a single overall rank. This approach can be applied to stocks you already own, stocks you think you might want to own, or the benchmark you're trying to beat, for example the FTSE All-Share or FTSE 100.

However, before I get into the details I just want to say that comparing investments by ranking them will only work if you have quite a lot of investments to rank. If you only have data for five or ten stocks then you could easily get misleading results. I would say that at least 20 stocks are needed before this approach starts to work, and more than 20 is better. Joel Greenblatt's system ranks the entire US market of about 5000 stocks, while the database that I use contains more than 200 stocks.

So how does this ranking approach actually work?

I'll outline the whole process first and then we can look at some examples.

To give each investment what I call a **defensive value rank**, these are the steps to follow:

1. Get the data for at least 20 stocks and, as I said before, more is better. This doesn't actually take a huge amount of time to build up; for example, jotting down the figures for one company each day will give you this much after 20 days. I always include the figures for the FTSE 100 in this list as well so that I am comparing stocks not only against each other but also against the market index I'm trying to beat. Treat the FTSE 100 the same as any other investment throughout the following steps.

2. Sort the list by growth rate from best to worst, i.e. highest to lowest. Give the fastest growing company a growth rank of 1, the second fastest a growth rank of 2 and so on.

3. Sort the list by growth quality from best to worst (highest to lowest) and give each a quality rank, with the highest growth quality company having a quality rank of 1, and so on.

4. Sort the list by profitability from best to worst (highest to lowest) and give each a profitability rank.

115

5. Sort the list by PE10 from best to worst (lowest to highest) and give each a PE10 rank.

6. Sort the list by PD10 from best to worst (lowest to highest) and give each a PD10 rank.

7. Optional: Sort by yield and give each a yield rank based on dividend yield (I don't do this, but you could if you wanted to focus more on higher yielding stocks).

8. Add together the growth rank, quality rank and so on to calculate an overall defensive value rank for each investment in the list.

9. Order the list by defensive value rank from lowest to highest, i.e. best to worst.

This may look like a lot of work but a computer program or spreadsheet can do it pretty much instantaneously. All you have to do is enter the required data, i.e. price, growth rate, growth quality, profitability and the ten-year average earnings and dividends figures (which are used, along with the share price, to calculate the latest PE10 and PD10 ratios).

One important point to remember with this approach is that a lower numeric rank is better while a higher numeric rank is worse. A rank of 1 is the highest possible.

Each company's defensive factors only have to be updated once a year after the latest annual results are announced, so it's probably a good idea to make a note of when the annual results are due (and for the FTSE 100 I update its defensive factors at the end of each calendar year). Spreadsheets, such as the ones you can find via the appendix, can be set up to automatically download the latest share and index prices, so once you have the data for a list of stocks to rank, the actual process of ranking them usually takes only a few minutes.

Once the defensive value rank has been calculated you'll have a list of investments which are ranked according to how well they perform, overall, across all of the defensive value factors. This is a much more flexible approach than the previous stock selection methods as it allows super-defensive but higher priced stocks to be compared directly to less defensive but much cheaper high yield stocks.

Here's my rule of thumb for using the defensive value rank, assuming that at least 20 stocks are being ranked along with the FTSE 100 or other market index.

Defensive value rule of thumb

Only invest in a company if its defensive value rank is better (i.e. numerically lower) than that of the market index.

So the underlying philosophy of this initial stock selection process is still to beat the market, except this time I'm looking to pick stocks where the combination of their defensive value factors, as measured through their defensive value rank, is better than the market.

By only analysing and ultimately buying stocks that have a defensive value rank considerably better than the market's, I expect my portfolio to have a better combination of defensiveness and value than the market. Over the long run that should enable it to achieve my targets of having a higher yield, higher growth rate and lower risk than the market (which so far it has).

In addition to the previous rule of thumb, I also want any new investment to improve my portfolio, which means I also use the following rule of thumb.

Defensive value rule of thumb

Only invest in a company if its defensive value rank is better (i.e. numerically lower) than most of your existing holdings.

This second rule of thumb only applies once you've built up a portfolio of at least 20 companies as otherwise it might be overly restrictive. However, once you have a mature and well-diversified portfolio, any new holding should be better than the average of your existing holdings. This means your new investments should improve your portfolio's average growth rate, growth quality and so on, rather than weaken them.

Let's have a look at an example and you'll see that this method is relatively straightforward in practice.

The defensive value rank in action

Table 6.3 shows the defensive value factors for some of my recent investments as well as the FTSE 100. They are shown in alphabetical order, as they were at the start of May 2015. There are too few investments in this list for the ranking method to be effective, but I wanted to keep it short in order to simplify the example. In the real world this list should include at least 20 companies that you're interested in.

Name	Share price (p)	Growth rate (%)	Growth quality (%)	Profitability (%)	PE10	PD10
Cranswick PLC	1,424	9.8	96.3	11.6	22.8	61.6
FTSE 100	6,961	2.0	59.3	10.0	14.8	34.5
Hill & Smith Holdings PLC	695	9.7	88.9	10.1	21.3	59.9
Mitie Group PLC	287	13.2	92.6	13.9	17.1	39.9
Petrofac PLC	874	30.3	85.2	28.6	14.0	37.0
Rio Tinto PLC	2,885	13.0	59.3	12.8	8.8	43.1

Table 6.3: Defensive value factors for multiple stocks and FTSE 100 as at May 2015

When the defensive value factors of multiple stocks and a market index are placed next to each other, as in Table 6.3, it can look like a wall of meaningless numbers. There is so much information that it's hard to take it all in. Simplifying all this data into a single number is exactly what the defensive value rank is supposed to do.

It's a fairly simple job to rank each factor in turn and the data from Table 6.3 produces the ranks shown in Table 6.4. This time the table is ordered by defensive value rank rather than alphabetically.

Looking at the ranks in Table 6.4 it should be easier to see that Petrofac has grown the fastest (growth rank of 1), the FTSE 100 has the lowest quality growth (quality rank of 6) and that Cranswick is the most expensive relative to past earnings and dividends (PE10 and PD10 ranks of 6).

By adding together those individual ranks we get a defensive value rank for each investment. Rearranging the table by defensive value rank shows us which stocks have the best combination of defensive value factors and therefore which stocks might be worth investigating in more detail first.

Name	Share price (p)	Growth rank	Quality rank	Profit-ability rank	PE10 rank	PD10 rank	Defensive value rank
Petrofac PLC	874	1	4	1	2	2	10
Mitie Group PLC	287	2	2	2	4	3	13
Rio Tinto PLC	2,885	3	5	3	1	4	16
Cranswick PLC	1,424	4	1	4	6	6	21
FTSE 100	6,961	6	6	6	3	1	22
Hill & Smith Holdings PLC	695	5	3	5	5	5	23

Table 6.4: Defensive value rank calculation for multiple stocks and FTSE 100

In this case Petrofac seems to offer the best combination, while Hill & Smith is in last place. Of course this doesn't necessarily mean that Petrofac is a better investment than Hill & Smith; investing is not that simple. But this is a useful way to decide which stocks to look at first.

Given these results I would perform a more detailed analysis of Petrofac first. If that company turned out not to be a suitable investment I would work my way down the list, analysing each company in turn until I found one I was happy to invest in.

Not forgetting, of course, that I would only invest as long as the company's defensive value rank was better than the FTSE 100's and also better than the rank of most of my existing holdings.

Calculating a rank-based target price

As with the first three stock selection methods, you can also calculate a target buy price for a company using the defensive value rank. The general idea is basically the same; you adjust a stock's share price until its defensive value rank meets your criteria, i.e. is better (lower) than the market index's rank and is better than the rank of most of your existing holdings.

Let's say I wanted to invest in Hill & Smith. It seems like a reasonable pick because its growth rate, growth quality and profitability are all higher than the FTSE 100's, so it certainly looks like a quality company on that basis (ignoring the fact – for now – that we don't know anything else about the company).

However, in Table 6.4 Hill & Smith comes bottom of the list. With a defensive value rank which is worse than the market index's the stock does not meet one of my rules of thumb. But we can easily change its share price to see what sort of price would be required in order for the company to rank well.

For this target price example I'm going to assume that I own all of the stocks in the list except Hill & Smith, which means that to meet my rules of thumb that company needs to rank in the top half of the table, ahead of half of my holdings and the market index. Remember that this list of six investments is not large enough for the ranking approach to work effectively, but for the sake of this example we can ignore that detail.

Unlike the earlier methods of comparing stocks, there isn't a nice equation we can use to calculate a rank-based target price. Instead we have to use trial and error, otherwise known as guessing, which goes something like this:

I know that Hill & Smith's target price will be lower than its current price, but I have no idea how much lower. A good way to begin is to start with half the existing price and then adjust upwards or downwards from there if required. So in this case I'll guess that Hill & Smith's target price is about half of its May 2015 price of 695p, so my opening guess will be a nice round 350p.

At 350p Hill & Smith has a PE10 ratio of 10.7, a PD10 ratio of 30.2 and, just out of interest, a dividend yield of 5.1%. Those PE10 and PD10 ratios would rank at 2 and 1 respectively, giving the company a defensive value rank of 16, which you can see in Table 6.5.

Name	Share price (p)	Growth rank	Quality rank	Profit-ability rank	PE10 rank	PD10 rank	Defensive value rank
Petrofac PLC	874	1	4	1	3	3	12
Mitie Group PLC	287	2	2	2	5	4	15
Hill & Smith Holdings PLC	350	5	3	5	2	1	16
Rio Tinto PLC	2885	3	5	3	1	5	17
Cranswick PLC	1424	4	1	4	6	6	21
FTSE 100	6961	6	6	6	4	2	24

Table 6.5: Defensive value rank calculation with Hill & Smith at 350p

By a stroke of luck – as this was my first guess – 350p is the price at which Hill & Smith just about makes it into the top three in this list. If 350p had resulted in Hill & Smith being either higher or lower than third place then I would have simply made another guess, perhaps half as low again or halfway between 350p and 695p, depending on whether the price needed to go up or down in order to meet my rules of thumb. Having made another guess I would have then recalculated its PE10 and PD10 ratios and then the PE10 rank, PD10 rank and defensive value rank for the whole group.

Once again, this sounds like a lot of work, but a spreadsheet can do all of these calculations and rankings automatically (although you still have to provide the guesses).

At this point we now have all the tools we need to quickly decide if a stock is worthy of a more detailed analysis. We have the defensive factors and other ratios for analysing, among other things, how quickly and profitably a company has grown, and the valuation factors for deciding whether or not its shares might be attractively valued. And we also have a variety of ways to combine those various factors, either using absolute criteria or by measuring a company's factors relative to those of other companies and/or the market average.

In Part 2 we'll turn to the task of analysing a company's operations and history in some detail. Our goal will be to discover if it has any competitive advantages and whether it is a potential value trap.

Before we move on though, here are the rules of thumb from this chapter.

Rules of thumb for combining defensiveness and value

- Only invest in a company if it meets a sufficient number of your pre-defined criteria.

- Only invest in a company if its defensive value rank is better (i.e. numerically lower) than the market index.

- Only invest in a company if its defensive value rank is better (i.e. numerically lower) than most of your existing holdings.

PART 2.
QUALITATIVE ANALYSIS OF A COMPANY'S BUSINESS

In Part 1 we looked at companies purely in terms of their financial numbers. That's an important first step, but I would never invest in a company having only looked at its accounts and little else. Like most investors, I want to know much more about a company than just its raw financial data.

Going beyond the numbers to look at a company's operations, industry and competitors can uncover many important facts that don't show up in the accounts.

It can also help from an emotional point of view. If the share price of one of your holdings falls by 50% and you don't know anything about the underlying business, you will – if you are like most people – be sorely tempted to sell.

If, on the other hand, you know a fair amount about the business, and based on that knowledge you feel that the reasons behind the

50% decline are temporary, you will be far less inclined to sell. You may in fact see the share price decline as an opportunity to buy.

Having said that, I don't think investors need to spend endless hours reading through industry magazines, visiting factories or trying to understand every detail of a company's operations. As Benjamin Graham put it:

> "A thing I would like to warn you against is spending a lot of time on over-detailed analyses of the company's and the industry's position, including counting the last bathtub that has been or will be produced; because you get yourself into the feeling that, since you have studied this thing so long and gathered together so may figures, your estimates are bound to be highly accurate. But they won't be. They are only very rough estimates."

We will be analysing a company's business with two main goals. First, to decide whether there is a significant chance that the company is a value trap; in other words that although the shares appear to be cheap, they are actually not cheap at all because the company has hidden problems. Second, we will look to see if the company has any competitive advantages and more specifically, whether it has any low cost and durable competitive advantages that will help it survive and hopefully prosper in future.

I carry out this analysis primarily through a series of questions which are designed somewhat like a checklist. Part 2 explains the reasoning behind each question and shows how I have applied them to some of my own investments in the past.

CHAPTER 7.

Value Traps

"Can you believe that in 1975 I bought Waumbec Mills, another New England textile company? Of course, the purchase price was a 'bargain' based on the assets we received and the projected synergies with Berkshire's existing textile business. Nevertheless – surprise, surprise – Waumbec was a disaster, with the mill having to be closed down not many years later."

WARREN BUFFETT

Companies trading at attractive prices are almost always unpopular. That's fine with me, as long as the unpopularity is caused by a minor problem that can be fixed quickly and cheaply. What I want to avoid are value traps – companies that are unpopular because they're heading into permanent decline or where a major crisis is about to explode.

In the book *Corporate Turnaround*, the authors Stuart Slatter and David Lovett outline a series of principle causes of corporate crisis and decline. After reading the book I thought the causes were so good I turned them into a list of questions and I now run through those questions with every company I'm thinking of investing in.

I use the questions to help me find operationally robust businesses while – mostly – avoiding crisis situations and other kinds of value traps. My rule of thumb here is simple, although much more subjective than those in Part 1.

Defensive value rule of thumb

Only invest if you are reasonably confident that the company is not a value trap.

Before I start asking these questions I spend an hour or so reading through the company's past annual reports and investor relations website. This gives me a general idea of the company's history, what products and services it sells, who it sells to, how it creates what it sells, its internal organisation and so on. I like to write down a summary of these initial findings to help me organise my thoughts and I refer back to and improve this summary throughout the business analysis process.

Once I'm fairly confident that I have a basic understanding of what the company does I'll move on and look for areas of potential weakness using these value trap questions.

The questions are phrased so that a *yes* answer is good and a *no* answer is less good, but not necessarily bad. Generally I avoid companies where there are more no answers than yes answers, but what really matters is the details of each answer and your judgment about what that answer means in terms of the riskiness of the investment.

There are 19 questions in all and they're grouped under nine major topics. In the rest of this chapter I'll go over them one by one before working through a fairly detailed example.

Management

1. Does the company have a clear and consistent goal and strategy and is it focused on implementing that strategy successfully?

Many problems stem from management errors. However, most of these are impossible to spot before a crisis emerges. Those that can be spotted in the accounts, such as high levels of debt or low levels of profitability, we've already covered. So here I'm looking for signs of poor management that haven't shown up in the accounts.

One sign of poor management is that the company doesn't have a clear goal or a defined strategy for achieving that goal. Or perhaps it has a clear goal and strategy but doesn't appear to be seriously focused on implementing that strategy successfully. Good management would make all of those things a priority.

The goal might be known as the company's vision, mission or purpose, but it shouldn't take too long to find in the annual reports. There will usually be a high-level goal statement on the company's investor relations website or in the annual reports which explains why the company exists.

Similarly, it should be easy to find a clear description of the company's strategy in its annual reports, as well as a progress update on what actions have been taken as part of that strategy and how successful (or not) they have been.

This task has become easier in recent years as companies are now required to include a strategic report section within their annual reports. The strategic report's goal, according to the Financial Reporting Council, is to provide shareholders with "a holistic and meaningful picture of an entity's business model, strategy, development, performance, position and future prospects". For the most part they do exactly that and I find these strategic reports very helpful when first getting acquainted with a company.

2. Does the company have an obvious core business upon which its goal, strategy and long-term future are heavily focused?

A sign of good management is that it focuses on and takes due care of the core business, rather than getting overly excited about endlessly entering new and unfamiliar territory. If a company is going to prosper over the long term it must focus on what it can do that others can't, or at the very least on what it can do better than anyone else.

In most cases companies can only do one or two things better than the competition and it should be fairly obvious what those things are. I try to avoid companies that are involved in lots of unrelated activities and which take a jack-of-all-trades approach to business.

Once again the strategic report, along with the rest of each annual report and the company's investor relations website, should be a good starting point for uncovering a company's core business. Some companies will also put videos and slides from presentations on their corporate websites. I find these useful for understanding a company's business, especially those that are larger or more complex.

Operational costs

3. Is the company in the leading group in terms of market share within its chosen markets?

Size can help to keep costs down. In many cases larger companies are able to provide goods and services more cheaply than smaller ones, which is one reason why I prefer to stick to FTSE 350 companies and only rarely venture into the world of small-caps.

However, regardless of size, I prefer companies that are in the leading group within their markets.

If you're lucky you will be able to find this information in the usual places – the annual reports or the investor relations website. However, many companies do not mention their market share and so you may have to search online, by typing something like "what is Vodafone's market share?" into Google or another search engine.

If you have no luck with that then you can look for a market share proxy, i.e. something similar to market share, such as the company's market capitalisation relative to its peers, or industry articles which repeatedly refer to the company as "leading".

Even without hard numbers, you should be able to get a feeling as to whether the company is a whale or a minnow in its most important markets.

4. Has the company had the same core business for many years?

Another way that companies can do things more efficiently and therefore cheaply is if they have a lot of experience in their core industries and markets. Given that we're looking at companies with a successful ten-year track record, the answer to this question is almost always going to be yes, but it's still worth asking.

This should be quite easy to work out by reading through the opening pages of the company's annual reports from this year, five years ago and ten years ago. It should be fairly obvious whether the company has had the same core business.

Major projects

5. Is the company free of large projects which, if they failed, could push it into a major crisis?

CEOs who take bold, bet-the-company decisions are often praised as heroes (assuming the bet ends well), but I'd rather not invest in a company that is making, or is likely to make, that sort of bet. While large projects can be exciting for investors, managers and employees, they usually come with significant risks if things go wrong.

As before, the best way to find out what the company is doing, or planning to do, is to read through the opening sections of the most recent annual reports.

6. Is the company free of the need for large capital expenses (capex)?

As we saw with the lemonade stand example in Chapter 3, some companies need to invest in assets (such as a lemonade stand) that they expect to be productive for more than a year. These are known as capital assets and the money spent on them is a capital expense.

There is nothing intrinsically wrong with companies that need to invest heavily in capital assets in order to maintain or grow their profits. It all depends on how much needs to be invested and, as we saw in the chapter on profitability, what sort of return those assets can provide.

Large capital expenses are mostly a problem when the purchased capital assets then have ongoing running costs. In those situations a company could invest heavily in capital assets (e.g. factories, warehouses, shops) in order to meet increasing demand when times are good, but when the economy and subsequently demand inevitably slows down, the high and relatively fixed costs of running those capital assets can be left inadequately supported by falling revenues.

An example of this is the UK supermarkets Tesco, Sainsbury's and Morrisons, which need to spend large amounts on developing and upgrading stores. When the economy slows down, those assets can struggle to generate enough profits to cover their fixed costs and the return on invested capital can collapse in a relatively short period.

Another example is telecoms companies such as BT or Vodafone. These companies need to invest heavily in physical infrastructure (phone lines, exchanges, etc.) before they can use that infrastructure to generate revenues. Again, if demand and returns on capital fall, the investment in those capital assets cannot easily be retrieved (if at all) and it may be better for investors if the capital investment had never been made in the first place.

You can find the capex figure in the investing activities section of the cash flow statement. There should be a section in the statement called "cash flows from investing activities" or with a subtotal of "net cash from investing activities" or similar, and in that section there should be an item called "purchase of property, plant and equipment" and perhaps another item called "purchase of intangible assets". The sum of these items is effectively the company's capital expense for the year. Alternatively, you may find that your data provider – if you use one – already calculates a figure for capital expenditure, in which case your job is a little easier.

Once we have a figure for capex we have to decide exactly what we mean by large capital expenses. My approach to this is to use the **capex ratio**. You can calculate it like this:

capex ratio =
ten-year average capex / ten-year average post-tax profits

As I mentioned earlier in the book, I use normalised post-tax profits, but you could also use adjusted or reported post-tax profits instead.

Once the capex ratio has been calculated I usually express it as a percentage (multiply the ratio by 100) and apply the following definition:

1. **Low capex** – The capex ratio is below 50%. About half of companies spend this much on capex.

2. **Medium capex** – The capex ratio is between 50% and 100%. About 30% of companies spend this amount.

3. **High capex** – The capex ratio is above 100%. About 20% of companies spend this amount, i.e. they spend more on capex than they make in profits.

It is the high capex companies I would rather avoid. High capex on its own probably isn't reason enough to avoid a company, but it should make you think twice, especially if the company has fairly high levels of debt and/or low profitability.

7. Are revenues generated through the sale of a large number of small-ticket items rather than through major one-off contracts?

Major contracts are another type of big project and they're the bread and butter of many companies, particularly those in the construction and support services industries. There is nothing intrinsically wrong with companies that generate revenue primarily through large contracts, such as building skyscrapers or running government prisons, but they do come with additional risks. This is especially true when the contracts are won through a process of competitive tendering.

The problem here is that because these large contracts are won relatively infrequently, and because each is so important to the company's success, there is sometimes too much focus on just winning contracts rather than winning profitable contracts.

The pressure to produce a competitive bid can lead companies to unknowingly underestimate the expenses they will incur whilst building or providing the contractually obliged product or service. The result can be a large contract which ends up making significant losses over many years.

Another problem with large one-off contracts is that they do not last forever. When they come to an end the revenues and profits generated by that contract need to be replaced, otherwise financial obligations such as interest and dividend payments may come under extreme pressure, possibly leading to rights issues and dividend cuts.

How do you know if a company depends on large one-off contracts?

It isn't always clear from the accounts, so you'll just have to read the annual reports, get a broad understanding of the company and then – in most cases – it will be fairly obvious. If it isn't obvious you'll just have to use your best judgment. Either way, you should make a note of your conclusions so that you can refer back to them when making your final decision about whether to invest.

I began asking this question after I invested in two companies which both subsequently suffered from problems with large contracts. The companies were Balfour Beatty and Serco.

Balfour builds bridges and other major pieces of infrastructure that take millions of pounds and several years to build, and those projects must be replaced with equally large projects when they come to an end. This absolute need to replace large projects – at almost any cost – was a major contributor to Balfour's losses and dividend cut in recent years.

With Serco, shareholders also saw major losses and a dividend cut. Serco operates – among other things – prisons, air traffic control centres and nuclear weapons programmes, primarily for governments. It had basically the same problem as Balfour Beatty; large, long-term projects that occasionally need to be replaced, under highly competitive conditions, with equally large contracts. In Serco's case some of those large contracts, from which it could not escape, effectively locked it into multi-year losses.

I managed to exit Balfour with a small capital loss that was offset by its dividend income, but with Serco I sustained a 50% capital loss and learned some important lessons. It was only my policy of broad diversification (which I'll cover later) that made the Serco loss a less painful experience than it otherwise might have been.

As they say, once bitten, twice shy, and I am now much more wary of companies that rely on large one-off contracts. However, that does not mean I wouldn't invest in that sort of company again. It just means that I would be extra cautious and perhaps require a higher standard than usual for other aspects of the company, such as its profitability and debt levels.

Mergers and acquisitions

8. Has the company avoided mergers or large acquisitions in the last few years?

Personally I have a mild dislike of large acquisitions and mergers as they can destabilise a company's core business. An acquired business usually needs to be integrated to some degree, especially if synergies and cost savings are sought. All of that can take resources and focus away from the all-important core business, which is rarely a good idea.

There is also empirical evidence to suggest that acquisitions are not generally positive for the acquiring company's shareholders as the price paid is often too high.

I'm not totally against acquisitions as it's a legitimate growth strategy. However, each acquisition should be small enough that it can't have a significantly negative impact on the acquirer's core business. That should be true even if there are integration problems and even if the price paid was too high.

Acquisitions can be found in the cash flow statement and in the notes to the accounts at the back of each annual report. If there have been any acquisitions then you'll find the amounts under the investing activities section of the cash flow statement. The name of that section may vary but it should definitely have "investing" in it. The actual amount will be called "acquisition of subsidiaries" or something similar with the word "acquisition" in it.

An accounting note associated with the acquisition will give you more detail, such as how much was paid per company, if more than one company was acquired.

So now that we have the amount spent on acquisitions we need to define what constitutes a large acquisition.

Generally I'm not worried about acquisitions as long as the company spent less in a given year than it made in post-tax profits. In other words, I use the following definition:

1. **Small acquisitions** – Total spent on acquisitions in a year is less than that year's post-tax profits.

2. **Large acquisitions** – Total spent on acquisitions in a year is more than that year's post-tax profits.

I look at each company's acquisition history going back ten years. If there is a large acquisition in that period then I'll have a closer look at what it was and how it has worked out (so far). I look for signs that the acquisition has caused problems or has significantly underperformed expectations. Either of those may indicate poor judgment on the part of management.

I'm also wary of companies that have made multiple large acquisitions in the last ten years, and if a company has spent more on acquisitions in the last ten years than it made in post-tax profits then that is a serious warning sign. The rest of the investment case would need to be extremely compelling before I would invest in such a company.

One example of a problematic large acquisition is Serco's purchase of Intelenet in 2011. Serco, as we've seen, provides services to governments through large, long-term contracts. As part of a push for diversification Serco purchased Intelenet – one of India's largest business process outsourcing (BPO) firms – for £385m from The Blackstone Group. At the time Serco's normalised post-tax profits were £180m while its average earnings for the previous few years were even less, so this was definitely a large acquisition.

For Serco this was also a strategically significant acquisition. It was a move into a new continent and a relatively new market (business services rather than government services). So how did the acquisition work out?

By 2015 Serco India BPO (Intelenet's new name) had grown its revenues fourfold, but that was not enough to stop Serco from selling the unit back to The Blackstone Group for £250m, crystallising a huge loss for Serco. In hindsight the Intelenet acquisition looks like a debt-fuelled lunge for growth at any price. This was particularly dangerous because Serco was already carrying significant amounts of debt and its ability to pay down those debts was – as we've already seen – dependent on its ability to win large contracts against committed competitors.

While the Intelenet acquisition was not the only cause of Serco's downfall, such a large acquisition was a good sign that management were willing to take significant risks in order to grow the business. As a defensive value investor, significant risks are something I would rather try to avoid.

9. Has the company avoided acquisitions that have little to do with its core capability?

As well as large acquisitions, those that are not closely related to a company's existing business can also be problematic.

This purchase of unrelated businesses is sometimes described as diversification, with hoped for synergies, cost savings and the opportunity to cross-sell into new markets. But often the result is an acquisition where the acquiring company is not the best owner of the acquired company. This usually happens because the acquirer has no special expertise or competitive advantages in the acquired company's industry. The result can be years of expensive integration headaches and a company that is more complex to run and less focused than it was before.

An example of this would be insurance giant Aviva's acquisition of RAC (the roadside repair company) in 2005. The idea seems to have been that Aviva would sell car, life and house insurance to RAC members, so effectively it was buying a list of names and addresses of people whom it could then market its services to. If these services were marketed under the RAC name to its members – the theory goes – they would be more willing to buy house insurance from the RAC than someone else. That may be true, but those customer names and addresses came attached to a roadside repair business; hardly an exact fit for Aviva whose core competencies must surely lie in insurance rather than repairing broken down cars.

In the end, the £1bn or so Aviva spent on RAC turned out to be an expensive way to distract itself from its own struggling core business. Various cost-cutting exercises were performed and subsidiaries were sold off, but the hoped-for synergies were not forthcoming. In 2011 Aviva sold RAC and more or less recouped its £1bn, but the distraction may have cost it much more than that.

Once again size is an important consideration, so I don't worry too much if unrelated acquisitions are small (as per my previous definitions of small and large acquisitions). But if they are large (individually or cumulatively) then this would be another negative factor against the company and another reason to be extra cautious.

Market demand

10. Does the company operate in defensive markets?

Some markets have highly cyclical levels of demand while others are less cyclical and more defensive. Companies that operate in defensive markets are generally less likely to see revenues and profits fall dramatically during recessions, less susceptible to industry downturns and less likely to be value traps than those that operate in cyclical markets.

In Chapter 4 we looked at whether a company operates in a cyclical or defensive FTSE sector. However, not all companies fit neatly into those sector definitions and sometimes the sector assigned to a company will be defined as cyclical when the company is actually defensive, and vice versa. As a result, I'll always spend a moment or two thinking about whether the company is best described as cyclical or defensive, regardless of what the sector definitions say.

Sometimes it can be difficult to decide whether a company is cyclical or defensive, but there are a couple of main points to look out for:

The terms cyclical and defensive refer primarily to levels of demand, so defensive companies are those where demand does not fluctuate widely. This means that defensive companies generally sell goods or services their customers need or want on a regular basis, where those customers are not willing to defer their purchase for any significant period of time.

These sorts of items are often referred to as small ticket, repeat purchase items, because they are inexpensive, frequent purchases. Good examples are:

1. **Soft drinks** – Such as IRN-BRU, sold by A.G. Barr, or R. White's (lemonade), sold by Britvic.

2. **Alcoholic drinks** – Including famous brands like Guinness, sold by Diageo, or Grolsch, by SABMiller.

3. **Toiletries** – Like Vanish stain remover by Reckitt Benckiser or Dove soap by Unilever.

These are products which most people are not willing to stop buying, even if there is a severe recession. There are other types of defensive product or service, but if you remember small ticket, repeat purchase you shouldn't go too far wrong.

Reckitt Benckiser is a good example of a company that is defensive in nature but is listed in a cyclical sector (the Household Goods & Home Construction sector). In my opinion Reckitt Benckiser should be in the defensive Personal Goods sector, but it isn't, which is precisely why it's worth coming to your own conclusions as to the cyclicality or defensiveness of each company.

Turning to cyclical goods or services, the easiest way to think about these is as the opposite of small ticket, repeat purchase; i.e. large ticket, one-off purchase. This doesn't adequately describe the offerings of all cyclical businesses, but if you're looking at a company that operates in a sector defined as defensive, yet its business involves selling products that are a large, one-off purchases (or at least infrequent purchases), you might want to re-categorise that company as cyclical.

Examples of large-ticket one-off purchases which are easy to defer are:

1. **Houses** – Housebuilders such as Barratt Developments or Bovis Homes are hugely cyclical and both of them cancelled their dividends during the Great Recession.

2. **Cars** – Car dealerships like Lookers and Pendragon can grind to a virtual halt during recessions.

There are other types of cyclical business too. Probably the second most common type is one where revenues can vary widely while expenses are relatively fixed. This includes:

1. **Restaurants and pubs** – Such as Enterprise Inns or Mitchells & Butlers, where rent and staff costs are relatively fixed but where it is easy for their customers to eat or drink elsewhere (or at home) during a recession.

2. **Mining companies** – BHP Billiton or Rio Tinto are well-known examples, where commodity prices and therefore revenues can fall or rise far more than the relatively fixed cost of supplying those commodities.

Having said all of that, it does not necessarily follow that a company operating restaurants or mines, or selling houses or cars, will be aggressively cyclical in nature. Some companies in these cyclical industries can ride out the ups and downs far better than others. But learning about the relative cyclicality of a business is still worth doing because it will prepare you psychologically for those ups and downs, if and when they arrive.

One last point on this is that, while it may seem that cyclical companies are just not as good as defensive companies, especially for a defensive value investor, this is simply not true. Cyclical companies, used in moderation and bought at the right price, can be a useful tool to boost a portfolio's returns. If you buy good cyclical businesses on low valuations at the bottom of their industry cycle, their share prices can improve dramatically when the cycle turns upwards again, and to an extent that defensive shares can only dream of.

11. Does the company operate in an industry where the pattern of demand (whether cyclical or defensive) is expected to stay the same?

In some cases it is not the degree of demand that changes but the pattern of demand. Customers may buy online rather than on the high street, or they may buy groceries in multiple local discount stores rather than in one big weekly shop at the out-of-town supermarket. The demand for the end product is still there, but the way in which it is bought changes and that in turn can have major consequences for the companies involved.

If a company operates in an industry which has the potential to be affected by large-scale changes (or disrupted, as it is often referred to) investors face the risk that the company will not be able to adapt competitively to the changing landscape.

Generally, low-tech products are more immune to changing demand patterns than either hi-tech products or services. For example, companies like Unilever or Reckitt Benckiser, which manufacture food, drinks, personal and household cleaning products, should be relatively – but not completely – immune to changing demand. At the other end of the scale companies like ARM Holdings, Apple or Facebook, are far more at risk from changing demand driven by technological or cultural changes.

12. Does the company operate in markets or industries where demand is expected to grow?

As well as cyclical changes in the amount of demand and periodic changes in the pattern of demand, I want to avoid markets where demand is in rapid decline.

The speed of decline is important because some markets are in a long-term contraction, but this could take several decades or even longer. For example, the market for fossil fuels is likely to be in long-term decline throughout the rest of this century. However, few investors think this will have any significant impact on oil and gas related profits within the next decade. The decline is so slow that its impact on current valuations is minimal.

On the other hand, the market for physical digital storage media, such as CDs and DVDs, collapsed so fast that companies like HMV and Blockbuster could not adapt quickly enough, rendering their shares worthless.

Product, service and price

13. Does the company generate most of its profits from products or contracts that do not need to be replaced in the next ten years?

The point of this question is to look for obvious and relatively major factors that could disrupt the company's revenues and therefore profits and dividends in the next few years.

If a company sells computer hardware (such as ARM Holdings or Apple) then we know, with near-certainty, that that hardware will need to be completely replaced within the next decade. Not slightly updated or tweaked – but completely replaced down to the smallest component. On the other hand a company that makes soap (e.g. Unilever) will probably only have to make minor changes – if any – to the shape of the soap or the design on the box. What it won't have to do is completely reinvent the concept of soap from its chemical constituents upward.

The most important thing for companies that need to repeatedly replace (or completely redesign) their products or services is not the capabilities of the current product, but the company's ability to come up with a successful replacement, over and over again. This is of course a much more difficult task than simply changing the colour of the stripes on a tube of toothpaste (which is pretty much all that Unilever has to do to reinvigorate its Signal toothpaste brand).

Another example is the pharmaceutical industry, where companies like GlaxoSmithKline or AstraZeneca can generate massive profits over many years from a single blockbuster drug. As long as the drug is protected from competition by a patent then wide profit margins and large profits can be maintained, but when the patent runs out the protection and profits can disappear very quickly. If a replacement product of sufficient scale cannot be developed then shareholder returns will suffer.

This idea also applies to companies that rely on large, long-life contracts. If a company is reliant on a small number of major contracts, but those contracts extend beyond ten years or so, then it may not be so much of a risk. But if those large contracts are due for renewal or completion in the next few years then there is a real risk that the company's revenues will be severely reduced if a replacement contract or renewal is not forthcoming.

This is basically what happened to Balfour Beatty and Serco, where major contracts came to an end and those companies were not able to effectively replace them. In both cases the results for shareholders were very bad indeed.

14. Does the company sell differentiated products that do not compete purely on price?

An important contributing factor for many companies that get into trouble is that they sell products or services which are commodities, i.e. they are virtually indistinguishable from the products or services of their competitors.

Commodity products compete almost purely on price, so a company that depends on commodity products for its success must have some sort of enduring advantage on the cost side in order to produce significant profits and high rates of return.

For example, Saudi Arabia is one of the lowest cost producers of oil and BHP Billiton one of the lowest cost producers of iron ore because they both own assets (oil fields, mines, etc.) which can produce those commodity products as cheaply as or cheaper than anyone else in the world. As a consequence they can match their competitors on price and still generate greater profits. Alternatively, they can remain profitable when prices are so low that other higher-cost competitors are going out of business.

So while selling commodity products isn't necessarily a bad thing, you should want to know if a company is dependent on them and consequently whether they have any enduring cost advantages (which I'll cover in the next chapter).

Commodity prices

15. Is the company relatively immune to commodity price movements?

Another uncertainty companies face is commodity prices. The price of oil, iron, copper and other commodities can be volatile, and the profits of companies who extract, refine and sell these commodities can also be very volatile. For example, when the price of oil goes up, companies that own oil assets and the companies that support them can be expected to do well, while the opposite may be true if oil prices fall.

What is perhaps less obvious is that companies in entirely different industries can also be affected by commodity price movements. An example here might be a company like Cranswick which – among other things – makes sausages and has expenses like fuel for tractors and feed for pigs. Both tractor fuel and pig feed prices will usually follow oil prices up – although they are somewhat less volatile than the underlying commodity – and so Cranswick's expenses are likely to go up with the price of oil. That in turn is likely to make its profits go down, unless it can pass on those increasing expenses to its customers by putting the price of its sausages up.

Of course, just about every company has inputs of some sort that are related to oil prices, even if it's only their electricity bill (unless the company uses 100% green electricity). So what this question is really getting at is whether the company will be significantly impacted by commodity price movements.

For example, ARM Holdings isn't going to be massively impacted by changing oil prices, even though it uses electricity and plastic in the production of its computer chips. On the other hand a company like Petrofac, which provides services to the oil and gas industry, may see a serious decline in profits if falling oil prices were to cause its oil company customers to cut back on their expenses.

Capital allocation and finances

16. Does the company have an expected rate of return on investment (ROCE or similar) of more than 10%?

As we saw in Chapter 3, any profits which are reinvested into a company still belong to shareholders. As a result management should at the very least expect to get a higher rate of return on that reinvestment than shareholders could get if they received the money as a dividend and invested it into an index tracker.

Historically the UK equity markets have returned something in the region of 5% after inflation, or about 7% if inflation stays near the Bank of England's 2% target. On that basis I think a management team that does not have an explicit goal for return on investment (ROCE or similar) which is in excess of 10% (to provide some margin of safety over the 7% minimum) is saying a lot about its attitude towards shareholders.

In other words, they are perhaps more interested in growing the company – even at low rates of return – in order to expand their own pay packets, rather than deploying capital in the most beneficial way for shareholders.

I think this goal should be prominent in the annual reports and clearly explained as it is central to the question of whether or not a company is being run well. Unfortunately, in the real world it is sometimes hard (or even impossible) to find.

17. Does the company's use of leverage still look conservative enough given the nature of the business and its environment?

If a company operates in a particularly cyclical industry, sells large-ticket items, has products that are about to become obsolete or sells into markets that are changing dramatically, it would be entirely reasonable to insist on an even more cautious balance sheet than is required under my various financing rules of thumb.

For example, I might decide – having looked at a company's operations in detail – that I would only invest if its debt ratio was below 3, rather than the 4 or 5 which I usually require. In more extreme cases I might insist on the company having net cash, i.e. more cash in the bank than borrowings.

However, if the company looks like a ticking time bomb then choosing not to invest at all is probably the most sensible course of action.

Current problems and final thoughts

18. Is the company free of current problems which could significantly reduce its earnings or dividends? If there are no major problems, why are the shares cheap?

The final step in this value trap analysis is to check the company's current environment for anything that is happening now, happened very recently, or is very likely to happen soon, which might materially and negatively impact its longer-term future.

These problems, if they exist, could come in almost any form. Generally I'll look through the company's most recent quarterly reports and then look at news on the company's website and from third-party outlets such as newspapers, investment or business-related websites and so on.

The best case scenario is a company that is having some sort of problem which scares other investors away and therefore makes the shares cheap, but where the problem is in fact relatively minor. By relatively minor I mean a problem that will have no lasting negative impact on the company's ability to grow its revenues, profits and dividends in the years ahead.

On the other hand, if I uncover something which could cause massive and long-lasting damage to the company (a very large fine, loss of licence, criminal charges, fraud, loss of a major customer, etc.) then I will probably move on to investigate another company instead.

19. Are the odds of this company being a value trap acceptably low?

This is the final and most important question; the point where you gather your thoughts and take a significant step towards either investing or not investing.

Sometimes the answer is easy. If a company has sailed through the questions with many more yes answers than no answers and with no obvious major problems today, it is not an obvious value trap. That's not to say that it couldn't still be a value trap, but only that it seems unlikely, which is about as strong a statement as we can make about the future of a company.

On the other hand, a company that has produced mostly no answers is much more likely to become a value trap and, as such, would perhaps be best avoided.

In between those two extremes are many more marginal cases, where it is not entirely clear (if it ever is) whether the company is a likely value trap or not. Unfortunately this sort of uncertainty, as opposed to the clarity of the quantitative approach in Part 1, is an inescapable part of business analysis. As an investor you just have to learn to live with the fact that in many cases you will have to use your best judgment.

These sorts of decisions can be incredibly difficult to make and are based more on gut feel and speculation than I am normally comfortable with. That's why, in most cases, I use these value trap questions to weed out companies where the risks are glaringly obvious, rather than marginal.

What constitutes glaringly obvious is impossible to define, but if a company gets more no answers than yes answers to these questions then I doubt that I would invest. Another example of an uninvestible company might be one where key contracts are about to end or where its industry (and the pattern of demand) is currently going through a major upheaval. In those cases I might also decide to end my analysis at that point and move on to look at another company instead.

However, if the risks are not glaringly obvious or if I only have minor doubts about a company then I'll generally invest anyway. Even if there is some element of doubt (as there always should be) then I can control the amount of risk I'm taking by keeping the position size of the investment relatively small (I'll talk about position sizing in more detail in Chapter 10).

Let's run through a fairly detailed example of this analysis process using one of my recent investments.

GlaxoSmithKline's value trap analysis

The following section is based on the notes I have from when I reviewed and subsequently bought GlaxoSmithKline PLC in January 2015.

I began my analysis of Glaxo with a general review of the company and its history, which I pulled together by skimming through the investor relations website and the opening sections of several recent annual reports. My goal at that stage was to understand, at a high level, what the company does and how it got to its current position.

After completing my initial overview I worked through the 19 value trap questions, again using information from the company's various annual, interim and quarterly statements, its investor relations website and of course other information on the internet.

Overview

Glaxo is one of the best-known Big Pharma companies in the UK and what it does is both very complex and fairly simple.

Its main business is:

1. Discovering new ways to treat health problems.

2. Patenting those discoveries.

3. Turning those discoveries into sellable products.

4. Getting regulatory approval to sell those products.

5. Manufacturing, selling and distributing those products.

The company operates primarily in prescription drugs and vaccines, but also has a growing consumer healthcare business that develops and sells brand-name products such as Beechams, Panadol and Sensodyne and makes up about 20% of group revenues.

Glaxo has a very long history in the pharmaceutical and consumer health businesses, having been created from the merger of Glaxo Wellcome and SmithKline Beecham in 2000. Both companies can trace their roots back more than a century to, among other things, Glaxo the baby food and Beecham's Pills, a laxative.

Having established a basic understanding of the business, I then moved on to the value trap questions. To answer each question I used a mixture of the company's website, its annual reports and the internet.

1. Does the company have a clear and consistent goal and strategy and is it focused on implementing that strategy successfully?

YES – Glaxo has had the same mission statement for many years, which is:

> "To improve the quality of human life by enabling people to do more, feel better and live longer."

In 2008 the company updated its strategy in light of changing industry and economic realities. The current strategy is:

Grow a diversified global business – To reduce risk Glaxo is focusing on diversifying its product offerings and moving into new regions, away from developed markets and towards emerging markets.

Deliver more products of value – This involves building the best product pipeline in the industry and focusing on producing high returns on research and development (R&D) investment. In 2010 Glaxo became the first pharmaceutical company to publish an internal rate of return on its R&D investment.

Simplify the operating model – This is a medium-term strategic goal to ensure the structure and systems in the business are capable of cost-effectively achieving the company's strategic goals.

As for clarity and focus, these strategic goals are a high profile part of the annual reports and it is easy to track the company's progress against these goals.

For example, in terms of growing a diversified global business, revenues from the West (US and Europe) are currently at 45% of the group total, whereas in 2007 they made up 78% of all revenues. In terms of delivering more products of value, the rate of return on R&D investment has increased every year since it was first published in the annual reports. In terms of simplifying the operational model, £3bn of annual savings has been found to date and almost £4bn is targeted for 2016.

2. Does the company have an obvious core business upon which its goal, strategy and long-term future are heavily focused?

YES – Glaxo has had the same core pharmaceutical business for many years, but it does also have significant non-core businesses. It is currently organised into Pharmaceuticals (primarily respiratory and cardiovascular; 67% of revenues), Vaccines (e.g. polio, tetanus, flu; 13% of revenues) and Consumer Healthcare (e.g. Horlicks, Sensodyne and NiQuitin; 20% of revenues).

3. Is the company in the leading group in terms of market share within its chosen markets?

YES – Glaxo is the world's sixth largest pharmaceutical company, the world leader in respiratory medicines, the second largest in over-the-counter medicines, the third largest in oral healthcare and it has a very strong global position in HIV treatments. It also has many market-leading individual products.

4. Has the company had the same core business for many years?

YES – Glaxo's predecessor companies (Glaxo Wellcome and SmithKline Beecham) have been in the pharmaceutical and consumer healthcare businesses for more than a century.

5. Is the company free of large projects which, if they failed, could push it into a major crisis?

YES – Over the past five years or so Glaxo has been working through a series of extensive projects to fulfil the strategic goals outlined in the answer to question one. These projects do come with risks attached, but after five years they have not induced a crisis yet and I think they're unlikely to. I could not see any other obvious large projects which would put the core business in jeopardy.

6. Is the company free of the need for large capital expenses (capex)?

YES – The company spends heavily on product research and development, but most of this is recorded as an expense on the income statement rather than as a capital expense on the balance sheet (i.e. the accounts assume that the money has been spent with no expectation of it having any measurable future value).

However, some R&D expenses are capitalised. Over the period from 2005 to 2014, Glaxo recorded a total capital expenses figure of £16.8bn, while its total normalised post-tax profit came to £47.4bn. This gives the company a capex ratio of 35%. As this is below 50% I would categorise Glaxo as a low capex company.

7. Are revenues generated through the sale of a large number of small-ticket items rather than through major one-off contracts?

YES – Although Glaxo does enter into some high-volume contracts with governments, these are relatively small for a company of this size. The bulk of its sales seem to come in the form of smaller purchases by hospitals, GPs and similar entities.

8. Has the company avoided mergers or large acquisitions in the last few years?

YES – Glaxo has been acquiring companies consistently over the years, but even the large acquisitions – such as Human Genome Sciences for £2.5bn – cost less than a single year's post-tax profit, which means they have all been small acquisitions by my definition.

9. Has the company avoided large acquisitions that have little to do with its core capability?

YES – Although I am no expert, as far as I can tell every acquisition over the last decade has been closely related to the company's core pharmaceutical and consumer healthcare businesses.

10. Does the company operate in defensive markets?

YES – Glaxo is a member of the Pharmaceuticals & Biotechnology sector, which is defined as defensive in the Capita Dividend Monitor. That categorisation seems to be correct as both the pharmaceutical and consumer healthcare markets have relatively steady demand over time and are largely unaffected by the wider economic environment.

11. Does the company operate in markets where the pattern of demand (whether cyclical or defensive) is expected to stay the same?

YES – Currently there are significant cost pressures from governments in the wake of the financial crisis, but the company still expects the pattern of demand to remain relatively unchanged for the foreseeable future.

12. Does the company operate in markets where demand is expected to grow?

YES – One of the key features of Glaxo's evolution over the last five years or so is its move towards emerging markets rather than its traditional developed Western markets. These emerging markets are growing at a faster rate and are expected to continue to do so for many years. As a global company it hopes to benefit from the world's rising population and living standards.

Glaxo has also changed which markets it focuses on and to what degree. It looks like the focus for growth will now be on vaccines and consumer healthcare more than pharmaceuticals, although the company expects global demand in all these areas to continue to rise.

13. Does the company generate most of its profits from products or contracts that do not need to be replaced in the next ten years?

NO – As a pharmaceutical company Glaxo generates most of its revenues and earnings from various medicine and vaccine products. The company's basic business model is to spend billions developing new products which – after proving successful in testing and acquiring regulatory approval – are then protected by patents. In turn those patents give the company a monopoly over a particular technical solution which allows it to generate high profit margins, even after taking into account the upfront cost of developing the product (as well as the cost of any research that ultimately failed to generate an effective product).

Patents don't last forever though. Instead they usually last up to 20 years, after which anybody can manufacture an identical product based on the same technology, without having had the upfront cost of all that research and development. This brings in generic competitors who compete primarily on price, which drives margins to unsustainably low levels for a company like Glaxo. At that point Glaxo has to either enhance the product and patent those enhancements, or stop selling it and move on to something else.

If a pharmaceutical company has its most important patents expiring in the short or medium term, it is facing what is known as a patent cliff. Unfortunately for Glaxo, it has been struggling with a patent cliff for several years as the patents for many of its top selling products have either expired or will do so shortly. The technical complexity of some of these products means that even after the patent expires it can be years before copy-cat competitors have a major impact, but it is only a matter of time.

For example Advair, a major product which accounts for about 24% of the company's total sales, has a patent which has already expired in the EU and is set to expire in the US in 2015. Other big sellers like Flovent or Avodart have patents which have either expired or will do so in the next couple of years. At least 50% of the company's current sales are in this position so Glaxo will have to work very hard over the next five to ten years to improve and/ or replace those products.

That is where the company's pipeline of new drugs comes in. Pharmaceutical companies must have a good pipeline of new products in order to replace old ones as patents expire. Unfortunately I am in no way an expert in this matter.

However, as far as I can tell from my research, Glaxo's R&D efforts have been more successful in recent years than those of other Big Pharma companies. It has a number of major new products which are in the late stages of development or have recently acquired regulatory approval. These are expected to carry the company forward in the medium term, with the longer term taken care of by more new products which are in the early stages of development. This is why it's so important for pharmaceutical companies to have world-class R&D facilities.

Exactly how the new products will perform is something that cannot be known in advance, but the general consensus among analysts is modestly positive.

14. Does the company sell differentiated products that do not compete purely on price?

YES – Most of Glaxo's products are protected by patents which allow them to be sold at far higher prices than if those patents did not exist. This does not give the company total pricing power though, because it often needs to negotiate with governments in order to win approval to supply high-volume buyers such as the NHS.

15. Is the company relatively immune to commodity price movements?

YES – Although commodities are used during the manufacture of the company's products, Glaxo's patents and high margins mean it can probably absorb commodity price fluctuations with relative ease, or pass them on to customers.

16. Does the company have an expected rate of return on investment (ROCE or similar) of more than 10%?

YES – Glaxo is apparently the only pharmaceutical company which publishes both an actual and target R&D return on investment figure. The target is currently 14% and the 2013 annual report quotes the estimated rate of return on R&D as 13%.

17. Does the company's use of leverage still look conservative enough given the nature of the business and its environment?

YES – In the 2014 annual results Glaxo had total borrowings of £18.8bn and five-year average normalised post-tax profits of £4.1bn, giving the company a debt ratio of 4.6, which was fairly close to my limit of 5 for defensive sector companies. On a purely quantitative basis, Glaxo's level of borrowing was acceptable, but perhaps a bit higher than I would prefer.

However, although the company operates in a defensive sector where demand is relatively stable over time, it is subject to a sudden loss of earnings when patents expire. The need to constantly replace existing products is a significant risk factor, and one which was serious enough to make me think twice about investing in this company.

In the end these subjective decisions come down to personal judgment, in this case about how likely it is that Glaxo's pipeline of new products will be able to offset the revenue loss caused by the patent cliff. If the new pipeline is not successful then revenues and profits would fall and that debt ratio of 4.6 could quickly rise beyond 5 and into the debt danger zone.

My personal judgment was that it seemed likely that Glaxo's pipeline would succeed in largely negating the negative impacts of the patent cliff. As a consequence I felt that Glaxo should be okay with its current levels of debt, or if not that it would be able to reduce those debts in a controlled manner, without the need for rights issues or dividend cuts.

Having said that, I am always the first to admit that the future is an uncertain place, and I could be wrong. However, I was comfortable enough with Glaxo's level of debt, given the inevitable uncertainties.

18. Is the company free of current problems which could significantly reduce its earnings or dividends? If there are no major problems, why are the shares cheap?

YES – Glaxo was facing various problems and uncertainties in January 2015 when I carried out this review, in both the short and medium term. This was reflected in its dividend yield of 5.6%, which was far above the FTSE 100's yield of 3.5%.

One problem investors were concerned about was the sustainability of the dividend if the company's pipeline turned out to be insufficient to offset lost patents. There were also some concerns about sales practices after Glaxo was handed a £300m fine in China for bribing medical professionals and others to use and promote its products.

Another area of concern was the ongoing restructuring of the company. This included ongoing R&D cuts, a possible partial (but still multi-billion pound) IPO of its ViiV Healthcare HIV drugs business, not to mention a complex deal with Novartis to create a new consumer healthcare company, offload its oncology business and acquire Novartis's vaccine business. So much change in such a short period of time creates risk and uncertainty, neither of which I am particularly fond of.

So at the time of my analysis there was a mixture of unpleasant events and uncertainties surrounding the company. However, I didn't think it was obvious that the company's earnings or dividends would permanently decline as a result of these issues. Instead, they appeared to me to be the sort of problems that all companies must occasionally face: unpleasant, yes, but probably not permanently damaging.

19. Are the odds of this company being a value trap acceptably low?

YES – The odds of any company being a value trap are never zero. There is always a risk that a company could run into major problems, slash the dividend and spiral into irrelevance. In Glaxo's case I thought the major risks were the patent cliff and the large restructuring projects, and issues with either of those could potentially be exacerbated by the company's relatively high levels of debt.

If, for example, lost patents are not replaced on a sufficient scale then the company will probably see its revenues and earnings fall, which in turn will undermine the sustainability of the dividend. Alternatively, if the restructuring projects became overly disruptive to the company's core operations then that could also have a major negative impact.

However, I thought a more likely outcome was that Glaxo would replace most of the revenues and earnings lost from expiring patents, and that the restructuring would not significantly harm the company. There is also the possibility that everything will work out even better than that, but I don't like to be too optimistic.

In summary, I didn't think it was obvious or especially likely that Glaxo would significantly cut or suspend its dividend, or announce a major rights issue any time soon. As a result I thought the odds of it being a value trap were acceptably low, but far from zero.

Having completed the value trap analysis, the next step, assuming the company makes the grade, is to look for competitive advantages. We'll work through that process in the next chapter.

First though, here are the value trap questions used in this chapter.

Questions for avoiding value traps

Only invest if you are reasonably confident that the company is not a value trap after asking the following questions:

1. Does the company have a clear and consistent goal and strategy and is it focused on implementing that strategy successfully?

2. Does the company have an obvious core business upon which its goal, strategy and long-term future are heavily focused?

3. Is the company in the leading group in terms of market share within its chosen markets?

4. Has the company had the same core business for many years?

5. Is the company free of large projects which, if they failed, could push it into a major crisis?

6. Is the company free of the need for large capital expenses (capex)?

7. Are revenues generated through the sale of a large number of small-ticket items rather than through major one-off contracts?

8. Has the company avoided mergers or large acquisitions in the last few years?

9. Has the company avoided large acquisitions that have little to do with its core capability?

10. Does the company operate in defensive markets?

11. Does the company operate in markets where the pattern of demand (whether cyclical or defensive) is expected to stay the same?

12. Does the company operate in markets where demand is expected to grow?

13. Does the company generate most of its profits from products or contracts that do not need to be replaced in the next ten years?

14. Does the company sell differentiated products that do not compete purely on price?

15. Is the company relatively immune to commodity price movements?

16. Does the company have an expected rate of return on investment (ROCE or similar) of more than 10%?

17. Does the company's use of leverage still look conservative enough given the nature of the business and its environment?

18. Is the company free of current problems which could significantly reduce its earnings or dividends? If there are no major problems, why are the shares cheap?

19. Are the odds of this company being a value trap acceptably low?

CHAPTER 8.

Competitive Advantages

"The most important thing to me is figuring out how big a moat there is around the business. What I love, of course, is a big castle and a big moat with piranhas and crocodiles."

WARREN BUFFETT

Competitive advantages can make a company more profitable than its peers. This is good because, as we've seen, profitability is effectively the rate of return you get on any earnings which are not paid out as a dividend.

Competitive advantages can also help a company survive the inevitable tough times that come around every now and then. This is especially important for value investors because we often end up investing in companies that are attractively valued precisely because they're going through tough times.

However, competitive advantages are hard to build and can be even harder to maintain. Most companies simply don't have any and that's why so few companies generate high rates of return over prolonged periods of time.

Another reason to look for competitive advantages is to learn about why a company has been successful in the past. Doing this research should complement the previous research you carried out when answering the value trap questions.

The rest of this chapter covers how I look for competitive advantages using another series of questions, this time based on Pat Dorsey's excellent book, *The Little Book that Builds Wealth*.

Dorsey's framework is used extensively by Morningstar and consists of four main types of competitive advantage. When I'm researching a company I always like to think about whether or not the company has any of these traits, and to what degree. I'll cover competitive advantages in some detail here, but if you want even more detail then Pat Dorsey's book is a good place to go.

My rules of thumb for durable competitive advantages are simple:

Defensive value rules of thumb

Prefer companies that have durable competitive advantages to those that have short-term advantages or no advantages.

Prefer companies that have low-cost competitive advantages to those with advantages that are expensive to maintain.

I have four questions which are designed to uncover whether or not a company has a durable and defendable competitive advantage. Few companies are likely to get more than one yes answer and most will get none.

However, not having a competitive advantage is not necessarily a reason to ignore a company. For Warren Buffett it might be, because his preferred holding period is forever. In other words, he would rather not sell a company once he's bought it, in which case competitive advantages are critical if the company is to perform well over decades.

I, on the other hand, am not a buy-and-hold investor. I expect to be invested in a company for somewhere between one and ten years, and over that timescale a durable competitive advantage is less important (although still preferable).

This means that for me a competitive advantage is a nice-to-have rather than a must-have feature, and regardless of whether or not a company has any advantages, asking the following questions will increase your understanding of its business.

1. Does the company have any intangible asset advantages?

There are three kinds of intangible asset that really matter:

1. Brand names

2. Patents

3. Regulatory licences

In different ways they each help a company to be the go-to destination for a particular product or service.

1. Brand names

Brand name products or services enable companies to sell more at higher prices.

A customer may choose a product because they trust the brand; it provides a sense of certainty that the product or service will perform as expected. You might, for example, choose a Toyota over an identically priced, functionally equivalent car because Toyotas are generally thought of as being extremely reliable, whereas you might not have the same sense of certainty regarding the other company's cars.

A branded product may also be chosen because of other factors such as image, where the image represented by the brand (a BMW for example) is more acceptable to the customer than a functionally equivalent alternative (perhaps a Toyota).

Whether it's through trust, image, or some other factor, good brands give customers some reason to choose the branded option over alternatives, and that is often true even if the branded option comes with a higher price tag.

The downside of brands is that they can become damaged and a famous brand can quickly become infamous when things go wrong.

2. Patents

There are few economic moats harder to cross than a patent. A patent gives a company legal protection from competition, effectively providing it with a legalised monopoly and an enormous amount of pricing power by banning others from making products that are too similar.

This is useful in those situations, such as in the pharmaceutical industry, where it would not make economic sense to spend billions of pounds developing new products (such as a new drug) which could then be immediately copied by competitors.

So patents are very powerful, but they're not a panacea and there are downsides. For example, they have limited lifespans, so the attack of generic competition is only delayed, rather than removed. It can also be very expensive to protect patents in court. Competitors will often try to challenge the legality of a patent and infringements on patents need to be dealt with as well.

A limited lifespan is the biggest problem. It means that products protected by patent must be continually replaced with new products and new patents if generic competitors are to be kept at bay. Coming up with new patent-worthy products is both very expensive and very difficult.

The result is that patents in and of themselves are only short to medium-term competitive advantages. In the longer term the company's true advantage, if it has one, will come from its ability to develop new patent-worthy products or services. In most cases that will require a world-class R&D department (or the equivalent).

Another issue with companies that rely on patents for their profit is that they can become lazy, growing fat and uncompetitive as the easy money rolls in from existing patents. This may lead to underinvestment in the research side of the business; a situation that can carry on for years while existing patents keep generating large amounts of cash.

At some point the old patents will expire and the research department will become the most important part of the company. If investment in research has been weak for too long then the company may well find itself downsizing dramatically as revenues that were previously patent protected drop away with nothing to replace them.

So when you're looking for competitive advantages in a patent-dependent company, look at the research side of the business. Does it have a recent history of successfully developing new products and patents, and has there been a sufficient amount invested to keep the company's research capabilities on the cutting edge?

I will admit that these are difficult questions and the answers can be subjective, but they are still worth asking.

3. Regulatory licences

Some industries are much more heavily regulated than others. In many cases a company needs to be licensed just to operate in a particular industry. These regulatory licences are effective barriers against new competitors, although they do vary in how useful they are as economic moats.

There are many different forms of regulatory licence and they appear in many different sectors, from gambling to public transport and energy supply. An example of a company that benefits from a strong regulatory licence is Royal Mail, where a major part of its business operates as the sole provider of the UK's Universal (postal) Service. This effectively means that, in exchange for having to provide postal delivery services to all parts of the UK, that part of the business is protected to some degree by regulation.

As with patents, there can be downsides to licences as well. For example, many regulatory licences come with government decreed price controls which are designed to stop regulated companies taking advantage of their sometimes monopoly-like status.

On balance though I think regulatory licences do help, as they can insulate a company from the kind of intense competition which is normally associated with efficient markets.

2. Does the company gain an advantage from switching costs?

Switching cost is a term that refers to how easy it is for customers to switch or substitute one product or service for another. The cost here is not necessarily in financial terms, although it can be, but could also include costs such as time, effort and so on.

For example, our local supermarket is a Tesco, so that's where we get our groceries. If I moved house and Sainsbury's became our local supermarket then that's where we'd shop. I can switch from Tesco to Sainsbury's with only the smallest amount of hassle (such as working out where the baked beans are).

Of course there are other factors. At my previous house the closest supermarket was another Tesco, but it was a relatively small one. Slightly further away was a Waitrose, which was also quite small and also more expensive. Just slightly further away again was a very large, new and beautifully fitted out Sainsbury's. Despite being further away we chose to shop primarily at Sainsbury's because of the greater range of products and because it was just a nicer place to go.

But we were not in love with Sainsbury's and as soon as we moved nearer to a relatively large Tesco, we switched back. All of the efforts by Sainsbury's to woo us with its fabulously big store were scuppered simply because we could easily switch to an inferior but nearer Tesco store.

Supermarkets have tried to increase their relative low switching costs by introducing loyalty cards and voucher-based systems. This was a competitive advantage for Tesco for quite a few years because it was the first to use them on a massive scale, but most supermarkets use them now and so the advantage, and related switching cost, has more or less been eroded.

The problem of low switching costs hampers most companies, but not all. One example of a company with very high switching costs is Microsoft.

Millions of people use Microsoft's products because that's what they've always used and it's what most other people use. Microsoft users have built up skill and familiarity with their products, not to mention a huge archive of files which work best with Microsoft software. The bother of switching to a competitor's word processor or operating system, even if it were significantly better, just isn't worth it for most people. The effort required to learn the new software is usually just too big a barrier to climb, and in some cases files and software won't work on anything but Microsoft's products. So for the most part, existing Microsoft users stick with Microsoft even though it may or may not offer the best products.

This gives Microsoft a massive base of customers who will stick with its products for years and even decades, loyally upgrading to whatever new products or new versions of existing products Microsoft decides to create. Importantly, this happens without Microsoft having to go to the expense of developing the *best* software; it can effectively get away with software that is just good enough.

Another example of companies that have high switching costs and barriers to customer exit are banks. Switching from one bank to another is a major hassle for most people (or at least they think it will be), so they generally don't bother. Consequently, banks are largely saved the bother of having to develop best-in-class products (at least for their existing customers – the best products are often targeted at attracting and acquiring new customers) and can instead simply focus on not annoying existing customers to the point where they want to leave.

3. Do the company's products or services have a network effect?

Some products and services get better as more people use them. eBay, Facebook and Microsoft are all good examples of how the network effect works.

eBay, for example, is an online marketplace for pretty much anything. As more people go to eBay to buy things it becomes a more attractive place for sellers as they will be able to sell a wider variety of goods more quickly than if there were fewer buyers. In turn more sellers will draw in more buyers as there will be a wider variety of goods on sale and competition among sellers will keep prices down.

This positive feedback loop between the number of buyers and sellers is why eBay has been so successful. Once a critical mass of buyers and sellers was reached, eBay's competitors found it impossible to compete without an equally large pool of buyers and sellers.

The network effect is also an important driver of high profitability and often leads to a winner-takes-all effect within a particular market. In the case of eBay, people will buy and sell on eBay even if its transaction costs are higher than those of its competitors. The cost of the higher fees is offset by the ease with which almost anything can be bought or sold quickly and easily, due primarily to the large number of buyers and sellers. So eBay gets the benefit of both higher transaction fees and a larger number of transactions than its competitors.

Facebook is a similar situation, where the social network becomes more attractive as more people use it. For many people, time spent on other social networks is not as appealing because there are more people they know, and more people in general, on Facebook.

As for Microsoft, in addition to its switching costs it also has a network effect. Microsoft Word, for example, is popular not necessarily because it is a good word processor (which it may or may not be), but because millions of other people already use it. If you write a Word document and email it to someone else there's a good chance they'll be able to read and edit it because they already have Word on their computer. If you use a word processor that has very few users you could end up writing documents that your intended audience cannot work with.

4. Does the company have any durable cost advantages?

Being able to sell products or services for less than your competitors, while maintaining decent levels of profitability, is of course a great advantage. But as with most competitive advantages it's a difficult trick to maintain over time.

It's no good simply cutting costs to boost profits in the short term as that will likely undermine the company's long-term prospects.

It's also no good simply investing in newer, more efficient technology that enables the production of widgets more cheaply than competing widget manufacturers. If one company can do it then others can do it, and it wouldn't be long before every widget manufacturer had invested in the same technology to gain the same advantage. At that point they'd be back to competing on price, producing very little in the way of profit and a terrible return on their new technological investment (although of course the consumer would benefit from cheaper widgets).

Durability is what really matters and durable cost advantages come in four flavours:

1. Cheaper processes
2. Better (and cheaper) locations
3. Unique low-cost physical assets
4. Greater scale

1. Cheaper processes

Sometimes a company will come up with a new and cheaper way to do business in a particular industry. Examples of this are Dell, which has historically undercut its competitors by going around the middleman and selling PCs direct to customers, or Primark (owned by Associated British Foods), which built its business by getting catwalk fashion onto the high street faster and cheaper than anybody else.

A cheaper process creates a cost advantage, but most processes are relatively easy to copy. However, if you're the first in an industry to use a new process it can take years for your competitors to negate that advantage.

It can take years for competitors to catch up because it isn't always obvious that a new process is either sustainable or scalable (and sometimes it isn't even obvious what the new process is). As the process is new and hasn't been used before, competitors usually won't want to go through the pain and hassle of changing their existing business without solid proof that the results will be worth it.

As a consequence, companies that develop and focus wholeheartedly on a new, cheaper process can often grow significantly before competitors take any notice, and by that time the innovator has often cornered the market in their particular niche. That's what Primark seems to have done in recent years.

However, in the longer term (perhaps over ten years or so) these cheaper processes are replicable and so over time it's quite likely that competitors, both large and small, will copy what they can. Eventually the new process will be an industry standard and any competitive advantage derived from it will likely be gone.

2. Better (and cheaper) locations

A better location in this context usually means closer to the customer. A location can become a durable cost advantage when it's more convenient for the customer to travel a short distance to that location, and where it's too expensive for competitors to deliver from further away.

For example, if Tesco is the first supermarket to open in a town then its economies of scale can enable it to quickly dominate any existing smaller grocers. However, if there aren't enough local shoppers to sustain two supermarkets then it may not make sense for a competitor, such as Sainsbury's, to even try to open a store in the same town. Tesco would then effectively have a local monopoly.

Of course there are no guarantees and more recently the changing habits of shoppers – shopping online or using smaller convenience and discount stores – has undermined this cost advantage for supermarkets. Even so, the general principle that some locations provide unique cost advantages is still sound and locations cannot be replicated.

3. Unique low-cost physical assets

Whereas better (and cheaper) locations relates mostly to the point where products and services are delivered to customers, unique low-cost physical assets refers mostly to locations where raw materials are extracted from the ground.

If, for example, a company owns an oil field that has the lowest oil extraction cost in the world by a significant margin, then that company will be able to extract and ship its oil around the world more cheaply than its competitors. The oil field is unique and so cannot be replicated by competitors, and depending on the size of the oil field the low-cost advantage may last for decades.

Companies like Rio Tinto and BHP Billiton work hard to find and develop the lowest-cost deposits of raw materials in the world precisely because they want to have this competitive advantage.

4. Greater scale

Economies of scale are probably the best-known cost advantage and you can see it clearly in the massive superstores which exist in out-of-town retail parks. Having a single vast warehouse-like store that sells as much as ten or a hundred traditional stores can significantly reduce overheads from rent and payroll on a per-item-sold basis. Buying goods in huge quantities can also result in increased discounts from suppliers and may even enable some degree of control over suppliers (much like the power supermarkets have over dairy farmers).

However, being big is not enough. In order to use economies of scale as a competitive advantage a company needs to be bigger than its competitors rather than just big. Sainsbury's, for example, is a massive company with more than 100,000 employees. It has huge scale advantages over traditional grocers. However, its main rival, Tesco, is far bigger and has a clear scale advantage over Sainsbury's. It is no surprise that Tesco has historically had far better profit margins than Sainsbury's, largely because of its greater scale.

That doesn't necessarily mean a bigger company is a better company – there are many factors other than scale to consider – but size does often matter. If you're reviewing the biggest company in an industry then that company's size may be its most important feature.

Even if a company isn't the biggest in the industry, it may still gain a lot from being very big. Vodafone may not be the biggest telecoms company in the world, but the size and scale of its existing infrastructure is an effective defence against new industry entrants. Any company new to the telecoms industry would most likely have to sink billions of pounds into physical infrastructure before it could even think about competing seriously with Vodafone.

Let's revisit the Glaxo example and use these four questions to look for competitive advantages.

GlaxoSmithKline's competitive advantages

Here's what I came up with when I ran GlaxoSmithKline through these competitive advantage questions in January 2015.

1. Does the company have any intangible asset advantages?

YES – This is the key to Glaxo's competitive advantage and its ability to generate high rates of return (over 15%) on capital employed over a prolonged period of time. Its patents are intangible assets that increase profits from patented products. Competitors are unable to compete directly or exert much downward pressure on prices.

However, patents don't last forever and so the truly durable competitive advantage in this case would be the ability to repeatedly discover patentable medical solutions before others do. Glaxo may indeed have such an advantage in its respiratory business, where it has been a market leader for 40 years, but I'm not so sure about the other parts of its business.

Even so, I'm willing to accept that Glaxo's patents and ability to generate new patents do represent an intangible asset competitive advantage.

2. Does the company gain an advantage from switching costs?

NO – Customers (whether governments, medical practitioners or individuals) will generally have little trouble moving to alternative products if those alternatives have similar or better costs and benefits.

3. Do the company's products or services have a network effect?

NO – Glaxo's products do not become more effective as more people use them.

4. Does the company have any durable cost advantages?

NO – Running a low-cost operation is not a key part of being a research-driven pharmaceutical company, even though Glaxo has focused heavily on reducing costs in recent years. It is more important to have world-class research facilities, which can attract and retain the best scientific talent, than it is to strip costs to the bone.

From this analysis I would say Glaxo does have competitive advantages in its R&D facilities and patents. They may not be low-cost advantages, but given the company's long history of using this business model it is perhaps reasonable to say that these advantages are likely to be durable, at least over my expected holding period of a few years.

Let's have a look at another company, this time one with a very different competitive advantage.

Telecom Plus's competitive advantages

Telecom Plus operates in the Fixed Line Telecommunications sector (a defensive sector) and provides gas, electricity, mobile and fixed-line phone services and broadband internet to retail and business customers in the UK. It operates under the brand name Utility Warehouse and is a member of the FTSE 250.

I reviewed and subsequently bought Telecom Plus in May 2015. I've included it here as another example of what you might find when asking these competitive advantages questions. I'll start off with a brief overview of the company so that you'll have some background context to this analysis.

Overview

Telecom Plus (trading as Utility Warehouse) is the UK's largest independent energy supplier and has over 600,000 customers. Rather than being just an energy supplier, it is primarily a multi-utility provider, selling gas, electricity, home phone, mobile phone and broadband services to retail and business customers. The company's aim is to undercut its ex-monopoly competitors (e.g. BT and British Gas) on price while providing customers with the novelty and convenience of a single monthly bill and higher standards of customer care.

The company was founded in 1996 as a telecoms company enabling customers to access call rates that were cheaper than BT. In 1998 Charles Wigoder and associates acquired control of the company. Mr Wigoder remains as Executive Chairman today and still owns approximately 20% of the company.

1. Does the company have any intangible asset advantages?

NO – I don't think the Utility Warehouse brand name is an advantage as most people haven't heard of it because the company doesn't use advertising. Also, while there are regulatory barriers to the markets it operates in, the company repeatedly describes the environment as competitive, especially with regard to new entrants. This suggests to me that the current regulatory barriers are not especially hard to overcome.

2. Does the company gain an advantage from switching costs?

YES – Utility services are historically quite sticky, i.e. people stick with a provider once they have found one that is reasonably competent. In addition, Utility Warehouse provides greater savings when a customer buys more services from them. This is a clear incentive for customers to aggregate all of their key services (gas, electricity, home phone, mobile phone and broadband) with the company.

If a customer wants to move away, the first barrier is that switching is a lot of hassle (or at least is believed to be) and the second barrier is the potential loss of savings compared to having all utility services provided by Utility Warehouse.

3. Do the company's products or services have a network effect?

NO – The company's products and services do not get better for each customer as more customers use them.

4. Does the company have any durable cost advantages?

YES – The company's business revolves largely around being able to provide energy and telecoms services more cheaply than its major ex-monopoly competitors. To achieve this it uses two main strategies.

First, it does not build or own any significant amount of energy or telecoms infrastructure itself. Instead, it effectively buys energy and telecoms services from companies like British Gas (owned by Centrica) or BT and then relabels and resells those services as its own. This means the company does not have to focus on any of the technologically complex, capital intensive aspects of those businesses. It can instead focus on the second part of its strategy.

The second part of the strategy is to acquire and service customers far more cheaply than its ex-monopoly competitors. Doing this allows it to undercut the companies whose services it is reselling, because the savings it makes in customer acquisition and customer service more than offset the percentage fee it has to pay to the companies that own the infrastructure.

To acquire customers more cheaply than its competitors, Telecom Plus uses network marketing rather than advertising or a high street presence. This enables the company to have almost no upfront customer acquisition costs. Instead, it pays a revenue-based commission to its army of over 50,000 part-time distribution partners (i.e. sales people), who spread awareness of the company and drive sales through word of mouth.

To service customers more cheaply it provides a range of services from gas to electricity to landline and mobile telecoms, as well as broadband and potentially home and car insurance in the near future. This gives the company a much larger customer base than if it just resold gas services, for example. This larger number of customers (600,000 at the latest annual results), all managed through a single, super-efficient system, allows it to keep costs as low as possible on a per-customer basis. To take advantage of this shared customer service, customers get lower prices as they take on more services which also helps to maximise revenue per customer.

This advantage is not necessarily durable, but so far no other competitor has come close to replicating this low-cost model on this scale in the UK. On that basis, as well as the fact that utility services are generally quite sticky, I would definitely say that Telecom Plus has some sort of competitive advantage.

The end of the competitive advantages questions marks the end of the company analysis process. In the next chapter I'll discuss my thought process before I buy, and the psychological commitment that is required when investing in a company for a multi-year period.

For now, here are those competitive advantage rules of thumb and questions again.

Rules of thumb for competitive advantages

- Prefer companies that have durable competitive advantages to those that have short-term advantages or no advantages.

- Prefer companies that have low-cost competitive advantages to those with advantages that are expensive to maintain.

Questions for finding competitive advantages

1. Does the company have any intangible asset advantages?

2. Does the company gain an advantage from switching costs?

3. Do the company's products or services have a network effect?

4. Does the company have any durable cost advantages?

CHAPTER 9.

Making a Final Decision

"If you don't feel comfortable owning something for ten years, then don't own it for ten minutes."

WARREN BUFFETT

With the value trap and competitive advantage analysis complete, the task of looking at a company's accounts and its business has come to an end, at least for now.

In summary, we've looked at:

1. Whether the company has paid a consistently profitable dividend.

2. How quickly it has grown over a number of years.

3. How consistently it has grown over a number of years.

4. What sort of return it has achieved on the capital employed within the business.

5. To what degree the company uses borrowed money to fund its operations.

6. How cheap the shares are relative to the company's long-term earnings and dividends.

7. Whether the shares offer a sufficiently good combination of defensive and value features.

8. The likelihood that the shares are a value trap.

9. Whether the company has any (preferably low cost and durable) competitive advantages.

Having completed both the quantitative analysis in Part 1 and the qualitative analysis in Part 2, it is now crunch time. If a company has passed every test thrown at it and come through with flying colours, there is only one decision left: to buy or not to buy.

Although investing should primarily be a cold, emotionless process of analysing information and data, there will inevitably be an element of emotion to it as well. After all, it involves putting significant amounts of money into something that is inherently uncertain, which for most people will elicit a feeling somewhere between fear and excitement.

Rather than trying to supress all emotion, I think it's important to have some degree of emotional commitment to an investment in order to ride out the difficult periods which frequently occur.

If you invest for long enough you will see bear markets, dividend cuts and profit warnings, not to mention rights issues, scandals and more. To avoid jumping ship at the first sign of trouble – which usually means selling when the share price is depressed – it's best to have at least some level of commitment to stick with an investment through good and bad, within reason.

This sentiment is summed up in another quote from Warren Buffett:

> "I never attempt to make money on the stock market. I buy on the assumption that they could close the market the next day and not reopen it for five years."

Buffett is famous for focusing on what companies are doing in the real world rather than what their share prices are doing on the stock market. Being willing to ignore the stock market for five years after buying a company's shares gives him the same mindset as if he were buying the whole company and taking it private (which he has also done many times).

Just think about the degree of belief and commitment that takes; the idea that you might buy shares in a company and not be able to sell them for five years, no matter what happens. That's the sort of commitment I think it takes to be a good long-term investor.

I'm not going to suggest that you hold shares in a company for five years no matter what, because I certainly don't. However, having that mindset does make me focus on what's important.

Committing, in principle, to a five-year holding period motivates me to do a thorough job when analysing a company. After all, I don't want to be locked into a company that isn't going to grow over that period.

It also means I'm less likely to sell at the first sign of trouble. I will go into this topic in more detail in Part 3, but investors who sell when something bad happens, such as a dividend cut, tend to sell low, and selling low is not my idea of a good investment strategy.

As you would expect, I have a rule of thumb which reminds me of the importance of this commitment.

Defensive value rule of thumb

Only invest in a company if you would be willing to own the shares for at least five years with no option to sell.

So if a company passes the various rules of thumb, i.e. its various defensive factors and value factors are attractive, it has some competitive advantages and isn't an obvious value trap, then I will sit and think through what the next five years with this company might look like. If the thought of investing in the company for five years doesn't scare me off then I will invariably invest.

However, not all investments are so attractive or clear-cut. You may decide that the price should be a bit lower before you're happy to invest, in which case you could make a note of the target purchase price and put the company onto a watchlist. Or you may have a lingering doubt about a company and as a result you decide that it isn't suitable, even though on paper it is.

Whether the final decision is to buy, to watch or to ignore, the process of analysing a company and deciding whether it should join the portfolio is over.

In Part 3 I will turn to the wider topic of portfolio management and why that is just as important as good stock selection.

PART 3.
MANAGING YOUR
PORTFOLIO

Analysing company results and share valuations is of course just one part of the investment process. Just as important, or perhaps even more important, is how your entire portfolio is constructed and managed.

In Part 3 we will be answering questions such as:

1. How many companies will your portfolio hold?

2. How long will each company be held?

3. How much will you invest in each company?

4. What sectors will they operate in?

5. Where in the world will they sell their goods and services?

6. Under what conditions will a company be sold?

We will also be looking at portfolio maintenance because – in some ways – a portfolio is like a garden which needs regular care and attention if it is to fulfil its potential.

To keep a garden in tip-top condition, weeds must be pulled up and fast-growing plants trimmed back to stop them from dominating everything else. In much the same way, weak companies should be removed and rapidly growing holdings pruned so that they don't dominate the portfolio.

However, like gardening, managing a portfolio does not have to involve frantic activity on a daily basis. In my experience a couple of hours each week, with some variation, is more than enough to manage a defensive value portfolio.

In Part 3 we will cover all of this and more.

CHAPTER 10.

Diversify Wisely

"There should be adequate though not excessive diversification. This might mean a minimum of ten different issues and a maximum of about thirty."

BENJAMIN GRAHAM

Most people intuitively understand the need to diversify their investments. It is basically the old cliché of not putting all your eggs in one basket. If you invest in one company and it goes bust then you lose everything. If you invest in 20 or 30 companies and one goes bust then it's not such a big deal.

Wise diversification is about more than just investing in a number of different companies though, so through the rest of this chapter we will also look at how we can diversify both industrially and geographically.

Diversify across many different companies

Investing in lots of different companies sounds quite simple, but how many companies is enough? Obviously one company is not enough, but at the other extreme, trying to emulate an index like the FTSE 100 by holding 100 companies is going to be far too many for most people. There has to be some number of holdings between one and 100 where a reasonable balance exists between risk reduction and the effort and cost of running the portfolio.

From a theoretical point of view the optimal number is usually thought to be around 15 holdings. In my case when I first switched from funds to shares I held just ten companies in my portfolio. After a couple of companies went bust (I used to invest in much riskier companies than I do now) I realised that having around 10% of my portfolio in each company was far too much for me to sleep well at night. I gradually increased the number of holdings in my portfolio to 20, reducing the average position size to 5%, but I still felt somewhat uncomfortable having that much in each company.

Eventually I realised that the question of how many companies to hold could be answered, at least partly, with the following rule of thumb.

Defensive value rule of thumb

Keep each position small enough so that you would not be overly upset if one of your investments went bust.

So take a moment to imagine that one of your investments has just gone bust. If it made up 1% of your portfolio, would that upset you? Would it upset you to the point where you might do something you'd later regret, like selling all of your investments and moving into cash? What about a 2% loss or 5%, or perhaps even a 10% permanent loss? This is entirely personal but in my case I start to get uncomfortable when I think about the possibility of a 5% permanent loss from a single holding.

Having settled on a preferred maximum position size, the next question is:

How does a maximum position size translate into the number of holdings?

It's pretty simple really. With a 5% maximum position size, 20 holdings will be the least I should have. You can calculate a minimum number of holdings by dividing the whole portfolio (100%) by the largest position size you're comfortable with (5% in my case), e.g.:

100% / 5% = 20

However, I wouldn't want to hold just 20 companies. As their share prices bounce up and down it would inevitably and quickly lead to some holdings being below 5% and many others above 5%. What's needed is a margin of safety, where the default position size is smaller than the preferred maximum so that each holding has some room to grow before reaching that limit.

As is often the case when I'm looking for answers, I went back to re-read Benjamin Graham. In *The Intelligent Investor* he wrote: "There should be adequate though not excessive diversification. This might mean a minimum of ten different issues and a maximum of about thirty." Previously I hadn't considered holding as many as 30 companies, but I decided to give it a try in 2012 and I haven't looked back since.

With 30 stocks in my portfolio each investment has a default size of 3.3% (i.e. 1 divided by 30). This is the size I aim to start new investments off at, although in practice it can vary between 3% and 4% depending on how much cash I have on hand to invest.

With a default position size of 3.3% each investment can grow by about 50% before it reaches 5% of the portfolio, at which point it will begin to make me uncomfortable. However, in practice I usually let a holding grow to around twice the default position size, or 6.6%, before taking any action (which I'll cover in Chapter 13 when I go over my rules on selling). Given that most of the holdings in the portfolio have position sizes of around 3% to 4%, I am comfortable with one or two (and it is usually no more than that) being somewhere between 5% and 6%.

Holding 30 more or less evenly weighted companies means I can sleep soundly at night and enjoy the process of investing rather than being stressed out by it. I have also found that 30 holdings can be managed with almost no effort on a day-to-day basis, so I would definitely not consider 30 to be too many stocks for a private investor.

Exactly how many companies you choose to own is up to you, but here are my first rules of thumb for diversification.

Defensive value rules of thumb

Hold 30 companies, approximately equally weighted (default starting position size of 3.3%).

Don't allow any one holding to grow to more than twice the default position size (i.e. 6.6%).

To give you an idea of what a portfolio might look like if it followed those rules I've included a list of holdings from a virtual portfolio in Table 10.1. They are shown as they were in May 2015, in order from the largest holding to the smallest. This is a model portfolio which I've managed and written about since 2011 and it is essentially the same as my personal portfolio in terms of the companies it holds.

Weight	Name	Code	Index	Sector
5.6%	JD Sports Fashion PLC	JD.	FTSE 250	General Retailers
5.2%	BAE Systems PLC	BA.	FTSE 100	Aerospace & Defense
4.9%	Homeserve PLC	HSV	FTSE 250	Support Services
4.8%	Cranswick PLC	CWK	FTSE 250	Food Producers
4.5%	Hill & Smith Holdings PLC	HILS	SmallCap	Industrial Engineering
4.5%	IG Group Holdings PLC	IGG	FTSE 250	Financial Services
4.3%	Telecom Plus PLC	TEP	FTSE 250	Fixed Line Telecommunications
3.9%	Mitie Group PLC	MTO	FTSE 250	Support Services
3.9%	Brown (N) Group PLC	BWNG	FTSE 250	General Retailers
3.8%	ITE Group PLC	ITE	SmallCap	Media
3.8%	SSE PLC	SSE	FTSE 100	Electricity
3.7%	Reckitt Benckiser Group PLC	RB.	FTSE 100	Household Goods & Home Construction
3.7%	GlaxoSmithKline PLC	GSK	FTSE 100	Pharmaceuticals & Biotechnology
3.3%	Tullett Prebon PLC	TLPR	FTSE 250	Financial Services
3.2%	British American Tobacco PLC	BATS	FTSE 100	Tobacco
3.1%	Braemar Shipping Services PLC	BMS	SmallCap	Industrial Transportation
3.0%	Amlin PLC	AML	FTSE 250	Nonlife Insurance

Weight	Name	Code	Index	Sector
2.9%	BP PLC	BP.	FTSE 100	Oil & Gas Producers
2.8%	Admiral Group PLC	ADM	FTSE 100	Nonlife Insurance
2.8%	Standard Chartered PLC	STAN	FTSE 100	Banks
2.5%	Vodafone Group PLC	VOD	FTSE 100	Mobile Telecommunications
2.3%	BHP Billiton PLC	BLT	FTSE 100	Mining
2.2%	Rio Tinto PLC	RIO	FTSE 100	Mining
2.0%	Petrofac Ltd	PFC	FTSE 250	Oil Equipment, Services & Distribution
1.9%	Centrica PLC	CNA	FTSE 100	Gas, Water & Multiutilities
1.6%	Morrison (Wm) Supermarkets PLC	MRW	FTSE 100	Food & Drug Retailers
1.5%	RSA Insurance Group PLC	RSA	FTSE 100	Nonlife Insurance
1.5%	Tesco PLC	TSCO	FTSE 100	Food & Drug Retailers
1.2%	Serco Group PLC	SRP	FTSE 250	Support Services
1.0%	Chemring Group PLC	CHG	SmallCap	Aerospace & Defense

Table 10.1: A list of holdings from a defensive value portfolio in May 2015

The size of each holding varies from about 1% to almost 6%. This is simply the result of share price movements over the years. Shares that go down, or at least don't grow as quickly as the overall portfolio, will consequently have smaller position sizes. Those that increase in value rapidly will grow their position size relative to the rest of the portfolio.

The next aspect of diversification to think about – beyond how many companies your portfolio holds and the size of each holding – is how similar the companies are. For example, if a portfolio is made up of 30 shoe retailers, all operating in the same country, then the portfolio is not very diverse at all, despite the fact that it holds 30 separate companies.

One way to reduce this risk is to make sure your portfolio holds companies from a wide range of different industries and countries.

Diversify across many different industries

This doesn't have to be especially complicated. In terms of industrial diversification, all companies listed in the UK have a sector or industry assigned to them. This is complicated slightly by the fact that there are various organisations which use different descriptions and categorisation rules, but as long as you stick to using the same rules the basic principles will remain the same.

In my case I use the official FTSE ICB (Industry Classification Benchmark) sectors, which are the same ones I used in Chapter 4 to decide how much debt a company can have. Rolls-Royce, for example, is in the Aerospace & Defense sector.

Although almost all companies could be hit by a global economic slump, it should be fairly obvious that a company in the Oil & Gas Producer sector is going to be affected by different economic factors than a company in the Fixed Line Telecommunications sector.

My simple approach to diversifying across a range of different sectors is to put a limit on how many holdings can be in any one sector. Personally I prefer to have no more than about 10% of my portfolio in any one sector, so with 30 holdings that means a maximum of three holdings per sector. It also means my portfolio will be invested in at least ten different sectors. This is helpful in two ways:

1. A recession in one sector shouldn't have too much of an impact on the overall portfolio.

2. Investing in a wide variety of sectors should increase the chances that a downturn in one sector will be offset by an upturn in another.

Both of these factors came into play during 2014 and 2015 in my own portfolio as a result of the collapse in global commodity prices.

In the recent past I have owned BHP Billiton and Rio Tinto from the Mining sector, Petrofac from the Oil Equipment, Services & Distribution sector and BP and Royal Dutch Shell from the Oil & Gas sector. All of those companies and sectors are strongly affected by commodity price movements. Somewhat simplistically, if commodity prices are high their profits will be high and if commodity prices are low, profits will be low.

When the price of oil and other commodities fell off a cliff in late 2014, so did the expected profits and share prices of these companies. Fortunately, thanks to my policy of wide diversification, I only had a few percent of my portfolio in each company and no more than two companies in any of those sectors.

So the first point above, that limiting the number of holdings in any one sector (and perhaps keeping an eye on the number of holdings in closely related sectors), reduced the impact of the commodity price collapse to acceptable levels.

However, the second point also came into play and a good example of this was Cranswick, the maker of sausages and many things pork-related. By holding companies from many different sectors, I am forced to invest in many sectors whose prospects quite often move in opposite directions. The Mining and Oil

& Gas companies do badly when commodity prices fall, but companies like Cranswick from the Food Producers sector are likely to do well.

That's because, as we saw in Chapter 7, oil and other commodities are primarily expenses for Cranswick as it has to purchase fuel for tractors and feed for pigs (where the cost of feed is also dependent on the cost of fuel and fertiliser). As a result, falling oil prices translates into falling expenses, which leads to rising profits.

While BP, Shell, BHP and the other commodity-related companies suffered, Cranswick's prospects soared, as did its share price. Not only did Cranswick's success offset some of the paper losses from the commodity-related companies, but I was able to eventually sell Cranswick in October 2015 for a 135% total return in less than three years.

As that example shows, diversification is just as important for increasing returns as it is for reducing risk. With a more widely varied range of companies in your portfolio, there will be more opportunities to take profits as some sectors soar, even while others struggle.

My rule of thumb on industrial diversification is:

Defensive value rule of thumb

Invest no more than 10% (e.g. three out of 30 holdings) in any one FTSE sector.

Diversify between defensive and cyclical sectors

Investing in many different sectors is a good idea, but what if most of those sectors are cyclical? Cyclical sectors have their own individual cycles, but they also tend to be heavily affected by the general economic cycle. When there is a general economic boom, the shares of many cyclical sector companies do well, but when the economy falls flat those same shares can really suffer.

A portfolio that is invested heavily in cyclical sectors may well be diversified across many different sectors, but because they are cyclical sectors the companies, their shares and the overall portfolio may end up moving dramatically downwards during the next bear market. This undermines the main point of diversification, which is to reduce risk, especially when the investment backdrop is scary (such as during a major bear market).

For that reason I prefer to have at least 50% of my portfolio invested in companies from defensive sectors such as Tobacco, Beverages or Electricity. That way I can be reasonably sure that a severe recession won't impact my portfolio as much as it does the wider market.

Defensive value rule of thumb

Have at least 50% of the portfolio (e.g. 15 out of 30 holdings) invested in defensive sectors.

Looking again at the holdings in Table 10.1 and cross-referencing their sectors against the defensive/cyclical definitions in Table 4.1, it turns out that there are only 14 holdings out of 30 from defensive sectors. The portfolio in Table 10.1 is therefore breaking this rule of thumb, which means that if I were running that portfolio today I would be looking to sell one of the cyclical sector companies and replace it with a defensive sector company as soon as is practical.

Diversify across many different countries

Spreading a portfolio across many different sectors is a good start, and keeping it balanced between cyclical and defensive sectors is even better, but if most of those companies generate their revenues and profits from the same country they'll be affected by the same country-specific booms and busts. This will make the whole portfolio overly susceptible to the ups and downs of one country. Fortunately it's quite easy to get around this problem by deliberately selecting companies that operate in a range of different countries.

To do this I make a note of the percentage of a company's revenues which come from the UK (as a UK-based investor investing in UK-listed stocks, I'm mostly interested in not having too much of my portfolio focused on the UK). The best time to do this is near the beginning of the company analysis process, so that a company can be ignored for now if it is too UK-centric given the current composition of my portfolio.

Many companies show in their annual reports how much of their revenues and/or profits come from various geographic regions. This data is also available for many companies from data providers such as Morningstar and SharePad. If I can't find a figure for UK revenues from a data provider or the company's accounts I'll use a reasonable alternative. A company may publish revenue figures for Western Europe, for example, and I can then make a ballpark guess as to its UK revenues based on that.

Once I have the data for each existing holding and each potential new investment, I can apply my rule of thumb for geographic diversification.

Defensive value rule of thumb

Have no more than 50% of the portfolio's revenues coming from any one country.

The easiest way to calculate this is to simply average the UK revenue percentage (or for whatever country you are most likely to be over-exposed to) for all of the portfolio's holdings. If, for example, a portfolio had three holdings whose UK revenue percentages were 100%, 50% and 20% respectively, the calculation would be:

portfolio UK revenue = (100% + 50% + 20%) / 3 = 57%

That portfolio is too exposed to the UK, according to my rule of thumb.

A more technically correct way to calculate this is to factor in the position sizes (also known as the weight) of the individual holdings. If in the previous example the company that generated just 20% of its revenues from the UK actually made up 90% of the portfolio, then the portfolio's total UK revenue would of course be much closer to 20% than 57%.

However, while including weightings may be more technically correct, the added complexity probably won't result in any significant additional diversity if your holdings are fairly evenly weighted. In other words, in a broadly diverse and fairly evenly weighted portfolio a simple average is good enough, and will be much easier to calculate and therefore more likely to be used over the long term.

In terms of the holdings in Table 10.1, the average of their UK revenues is 46%, so that portfolio is adequately geographically diversified according to my rule of thumb. If it had average UK revenues of more than 50% then I might decide, for example, to sell an existing holding that was highly UK-focused and replace it with one that was more international.

When to apply diversification rules of thumb

While it might be possible to tweak a portfolio at any time so that it fits within these rules of thumb, I tend to use these rules only when I'm making a buy or sell trade. For example, if I like the look of a company in the Bank sector the first thing I'll do is look at whether I already own three banks. If I already have three banks in my portfolio then I would immediately move on to looking at another company from a different sector.

Another example might be if my portfolio had too much of its revenues coming from the UK. In that case I would avoid buying companies that were heavily focused on the UK. Instead I would look to buy a company with revenues coming mostly from elsewhere. Buying an internationally-focused company would then lower the portfolio's overall UK exposure.

Thinking about diversification early in the analysis process will save you a lot of time because you won't end up doing lots of detailed analysis on a company that ultimately isn't suitable for the current structure of your portfolio.

Now that we've looked at how to structure a portfolio in terms of how many holdings, from what sectors and so on, I'll outline in the next chapter how I plan my buying decisions in advance so that I always know what I'm supposed to be doing and when.

Here are those diversification rules of thumb once again.

Rules of thumb for portfolio diversification

- Keep each position small enough so that you would not be overly upset if one of your investments went bust.

- Hold 30 companies, approximately equally weighted (default starting position size of 3.3%).

- Don't allow any one holding to grow to more than twice the default position size (i.e. 6.6%).

- Invest no more than 10% (e.g. three out of 30 holdings) in any one FTSE sector.

- Have at least 50% of the portfolio (e.g. 15 out of 30 holdings) invested in defensive sectors.

- Have no more than 50% of the portfolio's revenues coming from any one country.

CHAPTER 11.
Buy Slowly

"All day you wait for the pitch you like; then when the fielders are asleep, you step up and hit it."

WARREN BUFFETT

To many people, the clichéd image of someone who invests in the stock market is the Gordon Gekko type: someone in red braces, frantically shouting "Buy!" or "Sell!" into a telephone (usually along with several expletives). The reality should be very different.

Sensible investors should stay as far away from that sort of frantic action as possible. There should be no quick decisions to be made and no sweat-soaked brow to be mopped as you battle with the market.

My favourite analogy for managing a portfolio is gardening, where things need to be done on a regular basis if the garden is to flourish, but there is rarely much need for speed or panic. However, before a garden or portfolio can be maintained it has to be built, so that's how we'll begin this chapter.

Don't rush the portfolio construction phase

Let's assume you have a large sum of cash which you want to turn into a portfolio of 30 defensive value stocks. This sum should be at least £30,000, as broker fees of around £10 per trade could otherwise be an excessive drag on returns. Let's also assume you want to get your portfolio up and running as soon as possible.

How might that work in the real world?

In my experience it usually takes five to ten hours to fully review a company using the approach detailed in this book. Of course, if you start looking at a company and it fails one of the initial quantitative rules of thumb then your analysis may literally last five minutes, but to review a company right through to the end of the competitive advantage questions will definitely take several hours. So let's assume you can spare ten hours each week, spread across several days, to do investment research. At that rate it's going to take you up to a week to review a company before you eventually buy it.

I think reviewing one company in full each week is a pretty good pace to work at for most people. If you have more spare time or more brain cells than most people then you might be able to fit in more than one review each week. However, I don't necessarily think that's a good idea anyway; you might burn yourself out or just get fed up with the whole thing.

Assuming it takes you a week to fully analyse a company then it will take you about 30 weeks to build up a portfolio of 30 companies (I say about 30 weeks because life is full of uncertainties). This may seem like a long time to build a portfolio, but I think most investors would do better if they took even more time over this important task.

Remember, investing is something that happens over many years; five years at the very least and more realistically it's something that should be thought of as a multi-decade endeavour, in much the same way as you might think about a buy-to-let property portfolio.

Most people wouldn't start off building a property empire if they needed all their capital back in five or even ten years. If house prices fell over that period (which they easily could) the investor could lose an awful lot of money. Alternatively, if the property portfolio was viewed as a multi-decade plan, as it should be, then the risk of loss is massively reduced as property prices are almost certain to go up over 20 or 30 years, and the probability of a successful outcome is massively increased.

The same basic long-term approach should apply to investing in the stock market just as much as it does to investing in the property market.

So taking 30 weeks to build a portfolio of 30 companies is nothing in the big scheme of things. It is barely more than half of one year in the pursuit of a financial goal which should cover at least the next decade.

To paraphrase a famous cliché:

A share portfolio should not be built in a day.

However, as I said, I think taking 30 weeks to build a portfolio probably isn't long enough. Time is needed to get used to a new strategy and a new way of reviewing companies. Time is also needed to build up a basic level of expertise which can then be expanded upon in the years ahead.

More generally, I think making one trade a week is too much. It might give you the impression that investing is all about action and that there is something to do every week. In reality, there is very often nothing to do on a week-to-week basis and investing often works best when the investor can embrace inaction rather than action.

Personally I would much rather start off on the right foot by creating a portfolio in the same way I intend to manage it, which means making buy and sell trades less frequently than once a week.

Taking a year or more to build a portfolio

Rather than buying well-researched stocks as fast as possible, which for most people will mean something close to once a week, I think most investors will be better served buying no more than one company every two weeks. This slower pace would stretch out the portfolio construction phase to 60 weeks – or just over a year – for a portfolio aiming to hold 30 companies.

Why take at least a year to build a portfolio?

There are several reasons.

First, it gives the investor time to learn about their new strategy, how the company review process works, what happens when something goes wrong with one of the portfolio's holdings (inevitably it will), their own reactions to the market's ups and downs, and all the little details that you can only understand by experiencing them over a period of time.

It will also get the investor's mindset pointing in the right direction. As we'll see in a moment, the approach in this book calls for making one buy or sell decision each and every month, alternating between the two. So if January was a sell month then February would be a buy month and March would be another sell month. I'll get to the reasoning behind that approach shortly, but buying one company every other week during the portfolio construction phase is a useful introduction to that sort of slow, plodding, metronomic style.

One last point is that taking over a year to build up a portfolio gives the early investments time to actually do something interesting. If, for example, you bought 30 stocks in your first month, what would you do the following month? You would have no more stocks to buy and it would be ridiculous to sell anything you'd only bought the previous month, so you would probably just sit there and do nothing. And the same would probably be true the next month and the next. The risk in this situation is that you'll get bored and switch out of a perfectly decent investment strategy just because there is nothing to do.

As you might have guessed, I have a rule of thumb for this.

Defensive value rule of thumb

When building up a new portfolio from scratch, add no more than one new company to the portfolio every other week.

In case you're wondering whether I followed this rule when building up my own portfolio, I more or less did, although I hadn't developed the exact rule at the time.

After spending the latter half of 2010 developing the initial version of this investment strategy, I sold all my existing holdings in early 2011 and started again with a clean slate and an account full of cash. I bought my first defensive value investment in March 2011 (it was BP, bought shortly after the Gulf of Mexico disaster) and then continued buying between one and three companies each month. By the end of 2011 I owned shares in 19 companies. In 2012 I slowed down to buying no more than one company per month until my portfolio eventually reached 30 holdings.

All in all it took well over a year for me to become fully invested and I think it was time well spent. I developed a habit – a rhythm

– to my investment process, and I always knew what I would be doing each month. That bedrock of regularity and certainty was – and still is – invaluable in something as uncertain and long-term as investing in the stock market.

Make buy decisions in the evening or at the weekend

One thing that trips investors up time and again is the buzz that surrounds the stock market. There are a million and one websites pumping out an endless stream of articles every day, constant news about this or that company going up or down and share prices updated every 15 seconds. None of this is conducive to sensible long-term decision making.

Something I have found helpful is to only make investment decisions when the stock market is closed, either in the evening or at the weekend. I heard this first from Greg Davies, head of behavioural finance at Barclays, and I think it's a good way for investors to filter out the noise and excitement in order to make better investment decisions.

Even if you complete your analysis and in principle decide to buy (or sell) when the market is open, try putting the decision to one side until later in the day, or leave it until the weekend, and see if you still feel the same way having metaphorically (or perhaps literally) slept on it.

The rule of thumb here is simple.

Defensive value rule of thumb

Only commit to buying or selling a company when the stock market is closed, either in the evening or at the weekend.

Buy or sell one holding each and every month

Once a portfolio is past the initial construction phase it enters the maintenance phase. In gardening the maintenance phase is where weeds are pulled up, plants that have grown too large are trimmed back, fruits and vegetables are harvested and dead plants replaced.

In the investment world, weeds are companies that have to be sold because they are no longer defensive enough; plants that have grown too big are holdings that have grown to the point where their position size is now too large; harvesting fruits and vegetables is the act of completely selling holdings where their share price is no longer attractive, and dead plants are companies that have disappeared and need to be replaced, either because of a takeover or bankruptcy.

For whatever reason, many existing holdings will end up being sold over the years, at which point they'll need to be replaced in order to maintain the desired degree of diversification. Given that buying and selling are going to occur anyway, I prefer to take control of the timing as much as I can so that I know exactly when my next trade will be.

That wasn't always the case. I only became aware of the need for a planned approach to buying and selling after a period of excruciating inactivity in 2010. Month after month I had no holdings which were obvious sell candidates and at the same time there was nothing that I desperately wanted to buy. As a result I made no trades for about six months. That might sound like a nice break from activity but the end result was boredom, and to combat that boredom I got into the unhealthy (both financially and psychologically) habit of watching the market value of my holdings every day.

What I needed was a planned maintenance programme, in the same way that a good gardener knows there are certain jobs to do at certain times of year, and I eventually settled upon a monthly alternating pattern of buying and selling.

This slow and steady approach to maintaining a portfolio can also help investors get into the proper long-term mindset. Specifically, long-term investors should be:

1. **Patient and disciplined** – These are probably the two most important traits for investors. The more patient and disciplined you are the better your results are likely to be.

2. **Alert but detached** – A sense of detachment is surprisingly helpful when everything appears to be going wrong with an investment. When you know that you have only one trade to make each month you're more likely to forget about the stock market on a day-to-day basis, which is usually a good thing.

3. **Focused on the long term** – Investing really is about years and decades rather than weeks and months, and having your investment metronome tick once a month is a good way to get used to the idea of thinking on that sort of timescale.

4. **Happy and interested** – A monthly routine should help most investors avoid boredom or overwork, both of which are threats to long-term investment success.

The associated rule of thumb is simplicity itself.

Defensive value rule of thumb

Once a portfolio is fully invested, alternate buying or selling one holding each month.

I find that making one trade each month is the Goldilocks trading frequency for me (not too fast and not too slow). It gives me something to look forward to each month, either reviewing a new company to buy or performing an autopsy on an existing holding which I have decided to sell. It also means I don't have to think about buying or selling companies during the rest of the month, which in turn means I can more or less forget about my investments and get on with the rest of my life.

Another bonus is that this approach stops me from making knee-jerk sell decisions if a company announces bad news, such as a profit warning or dividend cut. I don't allow myself to make a sell decision on an ad-hoc basis; I force myself to wait until the first week of each month, which is my designated *trade week*. By the time I get around to making a decision on what to do, any emotion – whether anger, fear or whatever – will usually have faded and I can decide what to do with that company – if anything – in a measured way.

Another reason for introducing this buying and selling plan is that it leads to each individual investment being in the portfolio for an appropriately long period of time. Each year six holdings are sold and replaced (there are six sell months and six buy months each year) out of a total of 30. This leads to an average holding period of five years, which I think is a suitable minimum for a long-term investor.

Of course in reality some holdings will be sold after a year while others will be in the portfolio for a decade or more (I'll cover the whys and wherefores of selling in Chapter 13), but on average they will be held for five years. This is ample time for each investment to produce a good return from dividends, a good return from the growth of the underlying company, and perhaps even a good speculative return from positive changes to market sentiment.

In practice the plan is pretty simple: if I buy a new holding in January I'll sell an old one in February. Then I'll buy another new one in March and sell something else in April.

This allows me to continually clear the cobwebs out of the portfolio, or as I prefer to think of it, to remove the weakest link. Typically I'll sell the holding that has the weakest combination of growth, income, quality and value, using the various defensive value factors we've looked at previously. I'll then replace the sold company the following month with something from the market that has a better combination of those factors, and which passes the value trap and competitive advantage tests as well.

To give you an idea of what this process looks like in the real world, Table 11.1 shows every one of my buy and sell trades during 2014 where a new company joined my portfolio or where an existing holding left.

The only exception to the monthly alternating buy/sell decision is February and March, both of which were buy months. This is because I had decided to take a slow route to expanding the portfolio from 20 to 30 holdings, and so occasionally I would have two buy months back to back to increase the number of holdings. March 2014 was the last such month.

Month	Trade	Company	Reason
January	Sell	Aviva	Least attractively valued holding
February	Buy	Reckitt Benckiser	Replacing Aviva
March	Buy	Petrofac	Bringing the number of holdings up to 30
April	Sell	Mears	Least attractively valued holding
May	Buy	Serco	Replacing Mears
June	Sell	AstraZeneca	Least attractively valued holding
July	Buy	Standard Chartered	Replacing AstraZeneca
August	Sell	Royal Dutch Shell	Least attractively valued holding
September	Buy	IG Group	Replacing Shell
October	Sell	Greggs	Least attractively valued holding
November	Buy	N Brown	Replacing Greggs
December	Sell	Imperial Tobacco	Least attractively valued holding

Table 11.1: Every buy and sell decision for my portfolio during 2014

As Table 11.1 shows, defensive value investing does not involve a particularly high degree of activity, despite being a so-called active investment strategy.

Top up existing holdings with caution

Generally I don't like to add new money to existing holdings. Whenever possible I prefer to invest cash – whether from dividends, new savings or anywhere else – into new holdings only.

However, that isn't always possible. If you have a new influx of cash then it may simply not be possible to allocate it all to a new holding which, after all, is only going to make up 3% to 4% of your portfolio.

In those situations adding to existing positions may be the most sensible thing to do, but I would urge caution. Many investors like to add to positions that have fallen in value. The logic here is that if a company was attractively valued at 100 pence per share, for example, then it must be even more attractively valued if the shares fall to 60 pence. That may or may not be true, but you need to be aware that repeatedly adding new money to an existing holding in order to top it up is a risky game.

I learned this lesson back in 2011. Luminar Group Holdings PLC was an investment I made when I used to invest primarily in small-cap deep value stocks (typically struggling companies that are extremely cheap relative to their net tangible book value), and it was one of the reasons I got out of deep value and moved over to defensive value. Shortly after I bought into the company the shares fell quite substantially. I thought the company was solid, so I topped up the position. The shares fell further, so I topped it up some more. In total I ended up investing the equivalent of about 20% of my entire portfolio's worth into that one company. Luminar eventually went into administration, the share price went to zero and my investment became worthless.

To avoid having that situation occur again I am now firmly against adding to or topping up existing holdings. However, if an excess of cash makes it necessary then I will abide by the following rule of thumb.

Defensive value rule of thumb

When adding to existing holdings, don't let the cumulative amount invested exceed twice the default position size.

In practice that might look like this:

1. I have a £100,000 portfolio and invest 4% in Company A (£4000 cumulative investment).

2. Company A's shares drop by 50%. I still think it's a good investment. The portfolio's value is still £100,000 (other holdings have grown which offsets the decline in Company A) and Company A's position is now worth £2000, or 2% of the portfolio. I invest another £2000 to take the position size back to 4% (£6000 cumulative investment).

3. Company A's shares drop by another 50%. I still think it's a good investment and the portfolio's value is still £100,000. Company A's position is now worth £2000 again (2% of the portfolio) but I will not top it up for a second time as I have already invested a total of £6000, or 6% of the portfolio's current value, which is quite close to the 6.6% limit (i.e. twice the default position size of 3.3%).

4. Company A's share price remains the same, but the other holdings do well to the point where the portfolio is now worth £200,000. I still think Company A is a good investment. Company A's position size is now 1% of the larger portfolio (£2000 in a £200,000 portfolio) and so I top it up with another £6000. This takes the position's value to £8000 which is 4% of the portfolio. The cumulative investment is now £12,000, which is 6% of the now larger portfolio and therefore just about allowable according to my rule of thumb.

This is actually a fairly simple rule to stick to and only requires that you keep a record of the cumulative total that you have invested in each stock, which is something investors should do anyway.

In many ways buying shares is the interesting and perhaps even (for some people) the exciting bit. However, as an investor you will spend the vast majority of your time simply holding investments rather than buying or selling them, so in the next chapter we'll turn to the topic of holding, which involves coping with a range of expected and unexpected events.

First, here are the rules of thumb covered in this chapter.

Rules of thumb for buying slowly

- When building up a new portfolio from scratch, add no more than one new company to the portfolio every other week.

- Only commit to buying a company when the stock market is closed, either in the evening or at the weekend.

- Once the portfolio is fully invested, alternate buying or selling one holding each month.

- When adding to existing holdings, don't let the cumulative amount invested exceed twice the default position size.

CHAPTER 12.

Hold Steadily

"What you need is emotional stability. You have to be able to think independently, and when you come to a conclusion you have to really not care what other people say. Just follow the facts and your reasoning."

Warren Buffett

Although the buying and selling of shares is the bit that gets all the attention, simply holding shares is what you will be doing most of the time. This holding stage will last somewhere between one and ten years for most of your investments, if you follow the approach laid out in this book.

Why is the holding period between one and ten years?

If you hold 30 companies and alternate buying and selling one holding each month then you'll end up selling and replacing six holdings a year. At that rate it will take five years, on average, to replace the whole portfolio, which means your average holding period would also be five years. Of course there will be a lot of variation between one holding and another, and few will actually be held for exactly five years. The exact holding period for any investment will depend on how the company performs and how its share price performs, but most investments are likely to fall into that one to ten year range.

So what actually happens on a day-to-day basis once you own a company's shares?

The answer is not very much; in fact I think most investors should ignore their investments most of the time. One of the quickest ways to reduce investment returns and increase stress is to constantly look for and react to short-term news; worrying about every profit warning or dividend cut, or getting excited about every upbeat set of results.

One of the best ways to stop yourself from reacting to every bit of news, good or bad, is to already have a plan in place which tells you what to do, so that you don't have to make it up as events unfold. This plan can be broken down into two main areas: tasks that relate to expected events and those that relate to unexpected events.

In this chapter we'll look at how to handle expected and unexpected events in turn and then have a look at some examples from my own recent investments.

Handling expected events

There are some jobs that need to be done on a regular basis and I break these down into weekly, monthly or yearly tasks. By doing this I always know what I'm supposed to be doing and as a result I hopefully won't miss any important jobs along the way.

Weekly task: Read the latest RNS announcements

Although I don't want to get caught up in the daily ups and downs of the business news cycle, I still think it's important for investors to stay reasonably up to date with their investments.

Rather than newspapers or other third-party sources of news, I get my news from the official Regulatory News Service (RNS), which many online stockbrokers and investment websites provide (including some of those in the appendix).

The important RNS announcements are the official quarterly statements: the annual results, interim results (also known as half-year results) and interim management statements (also known as quarterly results). When these results are published I read them to see how the company is progressing and then save a copy for reference.

For the interim management statements I'll usually take no other action because – most of the time – nothing significant has changed from the previous annual or interim results. When a company publishes its latest interim results I'll read through them, but again typically take no action. However, when it comes to the annual results I'll go into much more detail and do a full review of the company using the newly published financial data (I'll explain this process in a bit more detail shortly).

There are other news items not published as part of the official quarterly results cycle but which can still be significant. This could be anything from a merger to a major new contract, so for that reason I prefer to subscribe online to RNS announcements so that I'm updated daily. On most days there isn't anything interesting to read, so checking these announcements once a week rather than every day is probably frequent enough.

Defensive value rule of thumb

Read the latest RNS announcements for each holding at least once a week.

Monthly task: Revalue each holding

The most important task each month is either the sale of the *weakest link* holding or the purchase of a new holding.

In order to do this as well as possible I need up-to-date figures for each holding's defensive value factors. This is actually quite simple as a company's revenues, earnings, dividends, debts, return on capital employed, and so on, only change once a year. So the defensiveness factors, i.e. growth rate, growth quality, debt ratio and so on, only need updating once a year. It's also quite easy to re-calculate the value factors, i.e. PE10 and PD10 ratios (and dividend yield if you use that in your valuation criteria), based on the latest share prices once a month.

The obvious tool for this sort of work is a spreadsheet. In fact a spreadsheet can be set up to automatically update share prices, in which case this task would require almost no effort at all (see the appendix for a link to download just such a spreadsheet).

If it's a buy month I'll use a spreadsheet to calculate all of the various factors and then rank my existing holdings (using the defensive value rank method) against a watchlist that I maintain of around 200 companies. I have to recalculate the defensive value factors for the watchlist companies as well, which is where an automated spreadsheet really comes in handy. After that I'll run through the buy analysis process until I find a suitably attractive investment.

If it's a sell month I'll work through the same process and then select one holding to sell (I'll go through selling in more detail in Chapter 13).

Defensive value rule of thumb

Re-calculate the defensive value factors for each holding each month in order to carry out the monthly buy or sell trade.

Yearly task: Carry out a full review

I always carry out a full review of a company after its latest annual results have been published. The first thing I do is update the growth rate and other defensive factors using the latest results because these are used in each monthly revaluation. However, this annual review is also a good opportunity to revisit the investment case for a company to see if it still makes sense.

This review basically covers the same ground as the original buy analysis, although it typically takes far less time. I'll already have the revenue, earnings and dividend values for the last ten years in a spreadsheet from the previous year's review or from the original buy analysis, so all I have to do is update them with the latest figures. The value trap and competitive advantage questions have already been answered at last year's review or during the original buy analysis, so reviewing them each year is just a case of running through the questions again to see if anything significant has changed (and in most cases it hasn't).

Most of the time this annual review won't result in any action, but there are times when it might. Examples would include companies where the defensive factors have worsened to the point where they break one or more rules of thumb, or where the value trap or competitive advantage questions generated too many negative answers. In both of those cases I might be inclined to sell sooner rather than later, but an immediate knee-jerk sale would still be unlikely.

Defensive value rule of thumb

Carry out a full review of each holding after its annual results are published.

Handling unexpected events

When everything is going well, investing is easy. You invest in a great company, the dividend goes up 10% a year and the share price follows. You check the annual results each year and your heart is warmed by the endless flow of good news. Nothing could be easier or more satisfying. But investing isn't always like that. Sometimes dividends get cut or suspended, CEOs get ousted and share prices collapse.

A common reaction to bad news and falling share prices is to sell immediately in order to stop any further losses. When I worked as a mechanical engineer in the 1980s I was taught to cut out rusty metal in order to stop the rust from spreading, and many investors follow a similar policy of cutting out investments that disappoint.

Selling losers may seem like a sensible policy, but generally I prefer to avoid selling at the first sign of trouble. It does depend on the situation, so let's run through some of the most common bad events that can happen and why I usually continue to hold rather than sell.

Falling share prices

Whether the reason is obvious or not, a falling share price is enough to make some investors sell. That's especially true if they use a stop loss, which is an order for a stockbroker to automatically sell shares if their price falls below a certain level. Stop losses are often set to sell at something like 20% below the purchase price. The idea is to avoid catastrophic losses if you were somehow wrong in your initial assessment of the company.

I think this is a bad idea in most cases. Deciding to sell shares simply because their price has fallen is the same as letting the notoriously fickle and jumpy Mr Market tell you when to sell. This viewpoint is summed up in a quote from Warren Buffett:

> "Mr. Market is there to serve you, not to guide you. It is his pocketbook, not his wisdom, that you will find useful."

It seems strange to me that an investor would spend a few hours of their time coming to the conclusion that a company was an attractive investment, only to sell it in a heartbeat, based essentially on no information whatsoever, other than that its share price had fallen 20% below the purchase price. It is precisely this sort of buy what's going up and sell what's going down mentality that gets so many investors into trouble.

I realise stop losses are an attempt to limit risk, but I would rather control risk through diversification and buying quality companies than with stop losses. Many of the companies I have invested in over the years have at some point fallen more than 20% below the price I paid for them. In the majority of cases they have subsequently rebounded into positive territory, and many have gone on to be outstanding investments. If I used a stop loss I would have been shaken out of those stocks and ended up with a short-term loss rather than the excellent long-term profit I eventually received.

A good example of this is JD Sports, the high street sports fashion retailer. I bought some of the company's shares in March 2011 at 228p (adjusted for a subsequent share split) and in December of the same year they were trading at 143p, some 37% lower. If I had used a 20% stop loss I would have sold out for a 20% capital loss after less than nine months. Instead, I held on and in December 2015 I sold the shares for 1002p, which is more than 600% higher than the lows of December 2011.

The point I'm making is not that I'm some sort of genius for holding on to JD Sports, but that share prices often decline by 20% or more, and often for no good reason. If the company is fundamentally sound then any decline will, in most cases, be temporary.

Defensive value rule of thumb

Don't sell just because a company's share price has fallen below your purchase price.

Dividend cuts or suspensions

Many investors think a dividend cut is simply not acceptable. They have an unwritten rule that says they will immediately sell, no matter how small the cut may be. As with stop losses, I'm not a fan of this approach and I never automatically sell when a dividend is cut. In fact I don't even sell automatically when a dividend is suspended.

In my experience it's never obvious how things will work out a year or two after the cut. Of course, on the day of the cut the share price will usually drop and sometimes it will drop dramatically.

This is unpleasant, even for the most stoic of investors. However, I like to remind myself that I'm in this for the long haul by asking myself:

What will the company's revenues, earnings and dividends be five years from now?

In most cases the honest answer is that neither I nor anybody else has a clue. The company could turn things around (good companies often do), its industry could pick up or improving market sentiment could drive the shares back up with or without a growing dividend. It is usually impossible to tell.

On top of that, in many cases a dividend cut can be a good thing. It can give the company extra cash to work with, enabling it to invest for the future and fix whatever problems it may have. Often the CEO and executive team will be replaced and the new team will be far more willing to shake things up to get the company going in the right direction again. Investors who sell immediately after a dividend cut will miss out on any potential turnaround and subsequent share price rebound. It's also likely that they're locking in a capital loss by selling when the share price is depressed.

Once again I like to use the analogy of a buy-to-let property. If you rented out a mortgage-free house then you would expect a certain amount of rent and hopefully a certain amount of cash income (much like a dividend) after expenses. You might also expect that income to go up roughly in line with inflation and wages. However, despite expecting your income to increase over time, you probably wouldn't be very surprised if it occasionally dropped.

That might happen for a number of reasons. Perhaps the existing tenant leaves and it takes you a few months to find a replacement, and so during those few months you have no rent coming in at all. Or perhaps you needed to spend an unusually large amount on maintenance in one particular year in order to repair a wonky chimney, and those higher expenses reduce your cash income by a significant amount. Or perhaps you just needed to lower the rent to attract new tenants during a recession.

So if the rent did drop in one year, what would you do? Would you immediately try to sell the property as fast as you could, even if it meant locking in a 20% or 30% capital loss?

I don't think many people would. I think in most cases a property investor would just accept the lower income as par for the course; an inevitable but short-term setback on route to long-term capital and income appreciation.

Admittedly, the income from a company is less certain than it is for a property; there are many examples where dividends have been cut and, even after many years, the dividend and the share price have failed to regain their former level. However, I think the general principle still stands: a dividend cut on its own is not a good reason to automatically sell a company's shares. I would extend that principle to include dividend suspensions, although if a dividend is suspended I would be very likely to sell if it is not reinstated within 12 months.

Although I won't automatically sell when a company cuts or suspends its dividend, I do investigate the reasons why it has occurred. If the reason is clear, and if it may have relevance to other companies, I'll try to integrate any lessons into my analysis process in order to avoid similar situations in future (I'll cover the importance of learning from every investment in Chapter 14).

Defensive value rule of thumb

Don't sell just because a dividend cut or suspension is announced.

Rights issues

Another event that many investors dread is a rights issue. This is where a company issues new shares in order to raise new funds (i.e. equity capital) from investors. This equity capital will typically be required for two purposes: to make a major acquisition or to pay down debt and fund the repair of a damaged company. Making an acquisition is often a positive event and so the rights issues that cause investors to sell are the ones that are used to fix damaged companies.

If this happens with one of my holdings then I will usually stick with the investment rather than sell, but I rarely exercise my right to buy the newly issued shares. That's because I'm not willing to invest more money into a company that may have been badly run and which is not up to the standards I'm looking for. Instead I will usually sell the rights that I have been issued (i.e. the right to buy the newly issued shares in the company, known as nil paid rights) and reinvest the proceeds into a different company.

As usual I have a rule of thumb for this.

Defensive value rule of thumb

If there is a rights issue for negative reasons keep any existing shares but sell the nil paid rights.

Let's turn back to the real world again and look at the events that happened as I held some of my recent investments and my reaction to those events.

To make things interesting, rather than reviewing investments where everything worked out perfectly, I'll run through a couple of examples where things didn't go entirely to plan. Hopefully these examples will highlight the benefits of holding fast and not panicking compared to the common approach of jumping ship at the first sign of trouble.

Holding Aviva from 2012 to 2014

My investment in Aviva ran from early 2012 to early 2014 and it most definitely did not go smoothly. In fact it was a relatively bumpy and somewhat unnerving ride. Figure 12.1 shows just how bumpy it was as the company lurched from one problem to another.

Figure 12.1: Aviva's volatile share price during my two-year ownership period

These problems were not entirely surprising as I bought into the company when it had a dividend yield of more than 7%, and you just don't get that sort of yield unless investors think the dividend is going to be cut at the very least. However, it's one thing to accept the possibility of trouble and quite another to actually experience it with your own hard-earned money.

Things started to go wrong shortly after I invested when Aviva's CEO was effectively ousted as part of the shareholder spring of 2012. The company had a goal of doubling earnings per share by 2012 and that goal had been well and truly missed. Institutional investors were not happy and they made it clear that a new CEO would be required. Of course the CEO's departure did not have a good impact on the share price, which fell by almost 30% at one point. As I don't use stop losses I had to sit and watch the share price fall, fall and fall again. Regardless of how stoic you are, watching the market value of one of your holdings decline by a significant amount is never going to be pleasant.

This is a good example of where my rule of not using stop losses worked out. On the assumption that my analysis of Aviva was right, and that it was a good company going through some short-term problems, the falling share price alone was not a good enough reason to sell. In fact, with that assumption the shares were better value after the fall than they were before and selling on the way down would have been folly; so I held tight. During the second half of 2012 my patience was rewarded when the shares rebounded strongly from their lows, gaining almost 50% in just six months.

But the roller coaster ride was not over. In early 2013 the new CEO announced a near 50% dividend cut as part of his new strategy of cash flow plus growth (which, to be honest, sounds pretty generic to me). The market had been anticipating as much in 2012 when I first bought the shares – otherwise the dividend yield wouldn't have been 7.2% – and the market was right. Large numbers of investors sold and the share price fell about 20% below my purchase price for a second time, and for a second time I held fast rather than abandon ship.

This initial 18 months holding period was bumpy and the news mostly unpleasant, but I was able to stick with Aviva without much in the way of stress thanks to my rules of thumb:

1. Wide diversification meant that Aviva made up little than 3% of my portfolio, so its 30% share price decline only reduced my portfolio's value by 1%. Such a small amount was easily and completely swamped by the ups and downs of the other holdings.

2. My weekly reviews of announcements, monthly reviews of valuations and annual reviews of fundamentals meant I was relatively detached from each piece of bad news as it came out. Whereas many investors panic-sold when Aviva's CEO left under a cloud, and again when its dividend was cut, my pre-defined action plan and refusal to make decisions while the market was open gave me time to reflect on those events and ultimately choose to ignore them.

Eventually this patient approach was rewarded. In the latter half of 2013 the market finally began to build confidence in the company's new strategy and its share price began to rise consistently. By the end of that year the shares were up more than 70% from the lows of 2012.

Of course, there were no guarantees that things would work out well after the company cut its dividend, but in the end the share price did rebound quite quickly and eventually gained more than 50% before I sold. The end result was an annualised total return of almost 18%, although that result had more to do with luck than I would have liked.

Why did I eventually decide to sell Aviva?

I'll cover the process of selling in more detail in the next chapter, but for now I'll just say that it came down to a weakening combination of defensiveness and value. Aviva's reduced dividend and falling earnings had weakened its defensive factors (its growth rate, growth quality and profitability) and the increasing share price meant its valuation (PE10 and PD10) was no longer as attractive as it once was.

The important point is that I avoided selling at the time of greatest fear, and therefore avoided selling at a depressed price.

Another important point is that after this relatively turbulent investment I spent some time reviewing what went wrong with the company and whether I could have spotted the impending dividend cut beforehand. This is something I do after every investment (and which I'll talk about more in Chapter 15). In this case my post-sale review led to the addition of the combined ratio and the premium to surplus ratio to my insurance company analysis process. Both of those ratios would have ruled out Aviva as an investment from the start, saving me a fair amount of stress and uncertainty.

Holding Balfour Beatty from 2011 to 2015

When I purchased shares in Balfour Beatty in mid-2011 the company was still performing well, despite obvious headwinds in the UK and US from recession-like conditions and government spending cuts.

Although my analysis of companies back then was more rudimentary, it still contained most of the elements of my current approach, and after reviewing Balfour I thought the company stood a good chance of getting through the economic slowdown without any major problems. For the first couple of years after I invested that was true, but gradually Balfour became more risky and some existing risks, which I hadn't spotted, began to have a serious impact on the company.

Figure 12.2 shows that there is some element of truth to the cliché that profit warnings are like buses – they come in threes.

Figure 12.2: Balfour Beatty's trials, tribulations and profit warnings, 2011 to 2015

For the first year or so Balfour continued to perform well against a difficult economic environment, but by the third quarter of 2012 things began to change. The company announced that profitability would be below previous expectations and that its construction services unit would face a tough 2013. The shares dropped by about 20% but I didn't sell and the price soon recovered.

In 2013 the less than positive trend continued. In the 2012 annual results, published in March 2013, the CEO spoke mostly of resilience in tough times and of growth when the recovery came, but revenues and profits declined. The full-year dividend was still increased by 2% despite those declines. Shortly afterwards the company launched an action plan as a response to increasing weakness in its UK construction business. Further negative announcements were made during the rest of the year.

In 2014 things just got worse. The 2013 annual results (published in March 2014) were very bad, with underlying profits down by around 30%. I didn't have to wait long to have my resolve tested again as the 2014 Q1 statement announced the departure of the CEO. In response the share price collapsed by 20% in a just few days, but still I didn't sell.

In September 2014 the dividend was put under review and the Chairman stated his intention to leave once a new CEO had been found. Unsurprisingly many investors threw in the towel and the shares fell as far as 150p, down more than 50% from the 320p they had reached barely nine months before. And yet still I refused to sell.

So if I wasn't selling, what was I doing?

I was sticking to the plan. After each annual report I updated Balfour's defensive factors and each month I updated its valuation ratios. In both cases they indicated that Balfour still offered a more attractive combination of defensiveness and value than most companies and so, despite the tsunami of bad news, I held on, although occasionally I questioned my own sanity. As so often happens, the share price recovered strongly and gained around 60% over the following six months.

By the start of 2015 the company had found a new CEO who immediately launched a transformation programme to turn things around. In the 2014 annual results (published in March

2015) the dividend was suspended, with the expectation that it would be reinstated no sooner than March 2016.

After updating Balfour's defensive factors from the 2014 annual results, the combination of weakening fundamentals and a recovering share price reduced the attractiveness of its defensive value factors to the point where it was easily the weakest (i.e. lowest ranked) holding in my portfolio. That weakness, rather than any fear of suspended dividends, profit warnings or departing CEOs, was why I finally decided to sell in April 2015 at 232p.

Of course, this was not a successful investment by any measure. It returned a small net profit of 8.9% over three years and eight months, made up of capital loss of 9.7% which was more than offset by dividends of 18.6%. However, I had stuck to the plan of deciding to hold or sell based primarily on the company's defensive value factors rather than allowing myself to be buffeted by events. As a result I had avoided selling at 150p and, perhaps more importantly, reinforced the feeling that I and I alone was in charge of my investment decisions.

As with Aviva, I learned several lessons from this experience. These led, in part, to the addition of the value trap questions to the analysis process. They also led to a change in the debt and pension ratios to make them more conservative as an excessively large pension scheme was one of Balfour's main problems.

Once again, the key lesson in the context of this chapter is to avoid selling when everybody else is selling, which is made easier by following a systematic, rules-based approach.

Holding Mears Group from 2011 to 2014

Just to show you that life as a defensive value investor isn't all bad, here's an example of a more benign and successful investment.

Mears Group PLC focuses mainly on the repair and maintenance of social housing, so its customers are typically housing associations and local councils. From its beginnings in 1988 to the point where I bought its shares in 2011, it had been an exceptionally successful company, growing both quickly and extremely consistently.

I invested in the company for all the usual reasons, in that it had a record of fast and consistent growth allied with a share price that meant it was attractively valued relative to past earnings and dividends. The dividend yield, at 2.5%, wasn't exceptional, but the growth rate of almost 25% more than made up for that.

Figure 12.3 shows how this investment turned out to be a relatively easy ride, eventually producing a capital gain of almost 100% in just three years.

Figure 12.3: Mears Group share price from 2011 to 2014

During those three years of ownership, Mears grew its revenues by 71% and its earnings and dividends per share by 44% and 30% respectively. It added more customers, more staff and more contracts, which greatly expanded its pipeline of future revenues. In short, it continued to do as well as it had in the past, which is all I can ask of any company.

Even in this happy situation there were still bumps in the road. Figure 12.3 shows that in November 2011 the share price dropped dramatically, leaving me with a capital loss of more than 21% at one point. If I had used a 20% stop loss then I would have sold Mears at the bottom and locked in that capital loss, all because some other investors decided to trade their shares for 210p rather than the 268p I'd paid.

Why did the shares crash so far in one day?

It was the usual suspect: a profit warning. In the November 2011 interim management statement the company announced that, due to the government halving the Photovoltaic Feed-In Tariff, it would no longer be looking to fit and maintain solar panels. As a result its profits were likely to fall below previous expectations by around £2.8m, and approximately £2m spent on the possibility of carrying out solar panel work had effectively been wasted.

It would be hard to describe that disappointment as anything other than a very minor setback. It certainly wasn't something that would make me want to sell a company I'd invested in for the long term, especially if it meant swallowing a 20% capital loss.

So I held on and the investment worked out very nicely in the end. The company did well, the shares more or less doubled, and eventually I sold because the price went up so fast its valuation factors became unattractive.

Now that we have covered both buying and holding, in the next chapter I'll discuss the final stage of the investment lifecycle. We'll look at when it might be a good idea to sell and also when it might not be.

But first, here are the rules of thumb for holding steadily once again.

Rules of thumb for holding steadily

- Read the latest RNS announcements for each holding at least once a week.

- Re-calculate the defensive value factors for each holding each month in order to carry out the monthly buy or sell trade.

- Carry out a full review of each holding after its annual results are published.

- Don't sell just because a company's share price has fallen below your purchase price.

- Don't sell just because a dividend cut or suspension is announced.

- If there is a rights issue for negative reasons keep any existing shares but sell the nil paid rights.

CHAPTER 13.

Sell Deliberately

"The basic rules of building wealth by investing in stocks will hold true in this century or the next; it's still 'Buy low, sell high.'"

SIR JOHN TEMPLETON

The vast majority of what is written about stocks focuses on what to buy; what stocks are hot right now or what sectors and countries are going to be the next big thing. In many respects that's understandable as making a new investment can be exciting in a similar way to placing a bet at the roulette table (at least for some people).

However, despite this popular focus on buying, what you sell and when you sell is every bit as important as what you buy and when you buy. Most investors I speak to simply have no pre-defined selling strategy at all, or they follow one of the common strategies such as selling on dividend cuts or selling on bad news in general.

I think this is a huge mistake. Selling well is incredibly important and your selling strategy should be just as well thought through as your buying strategy, and just as rigorously applied.

In this chapter I'll describe the rules which make up my selling strategy and how I use them to control risk, lock in profits on successful investments and exit underperforming investments (which, despite all of the hard work which goes into analysing companies before they are bought, can still occur).

A pre-planned approach to selling

As you know I like to make one investment decision each month, selling the least attractive holding one month and replacing it the following month with a new and more attractive alternative. In fact I go one step further than just fixing the number of trades per month to one; I also fix the time of the trade to the first week of the month.

Having a preset time for making investment decisions means I can more or less ignore my investments and the wider stock market throughout the rest of the month. I still check the Regulatory News Service for each holding on most days, but that only takes a few minutes as part of my routine. For the rest of the day, and for most of each month, the stock market may as well not exist.

When the first week of the month comes around I already know in advance whether I'm looking to buy or sell. If it's a sell month I can concentrate on what I'm going to sell and why, and do so in my own good time rather than making rash sell decisions based on fear and uncertainty.

Deciding what to sell

In most cases sell decisions should follow the opposite logic of buying decisions. When I'm buying a company I rely perhaps 80% on the defensive value factors and defensive value rank outlined in the first part of this book and 20% on the value trap and competitive advantage questions outlined in the second part. My approach to selling is the same.

In deciding what to sell I will first and foremost look to get rid of the holding which currently has the weakest combination of defensive value factors and the weakest defensive value rank. However, I will also take into account other factors, such as the company's debt-related ratios, its dividend yield (generally I prefer to sell low-yield stocks rather than high-yield stocks) and its value trap and competitive advantage credentials.

This is where the annual review and monthly revaluations come in. During each annual review I will update all of the quantitative factors such as growth rate, growth quality and so on. These will then remain unchanged for the rest of that company's financial year. I also work through the value trap and competitive advantage questions to see if anything significant has changed. During each monthly revaluation I'll update every company's PE10, PD10 and dividend yield ratios so I always have the correct information to hand in order to start the process of deciding which shares to sell.

I would say that whatever system you use for comparing companies in order to decide which ones to buy, use the same system for selling, but in reverse. If you buy stocks only when their defensive value factors beat the market, choose which holding to sell from those that beat the market by the fewest factors. If you use your own pre-defined criteria, choose which holding to sell from those that meet the fewest.

You could choose to just mechanically sell the holding with the weakest combination of factors, where weakest is defined by whichever stock selection method you use. However, I don't like to be completely mechanical with my decisions, so generally I'll look at the five weakest (in my case lowest ranked) holdings. I'll then pick which one I'm going to sell from that group after taking into account a range of additional factors such as their yields, their current situations and perhaps even my thoughts about their prospects for the future. This approach gives me enough flexibility so that I feel like I am making the decision rather than the system, but not so much that I'm at risk of making it up as I go along.

I might, for example, decide that the company ranked 27th out of 30 is in fact the weakest holding, perhaps because I'm unsure about the long-term future of its industry. That's a personal judgment rather than something which can be calculated from the company's accounts, but it would still be entirely reasonable to sell that holding rather than the one with the weakest rank. In making that decision I am being guided by the numbers but not completely controlled by them. I think it's psychologically important to feel like you have the final say, rather than a spreadsheet.

So now we've seen an overview of the selling process, let's look at some specific reasons why a company might be sold.

1. A rapidly increasing share price leads to weakening valuation factors

Sometimes, with a bit of luck, the share price of one of your investments will go up far faster than the fundamentals of the underlying company. If that happens, its PE10 and PD10 ratios will rise and its dividend yield will fall. If the company's defensive factors of growth rate, growth quality and so on are essentially unchanged, then its weakening valuation factors will make it less attractive as an investment. At some point what was once an attractive stock that you were happy to buy may become one of the least attractively valued holdings in your portfolio.

At that point it can often make sense to sell, even though the underlying company continues to be successful. Selling good companies at high valuations – or at least at valuations that are no longer attractive – makes sense because they will typically not have attractive dividend yields and the increased valuation ratios lead to an increase in valuation risk, which is the risk of the valuation ratios (and share price) falling back down again, even if the company continues to do well.

Selling N Brown after rapid share price gains

An example from my own portfolio of selling after rapid share price gains is N Brown, the home catalogue and online fashion retailer. I bought the company's shares in 2012 at 242p when they looked attractively valued. The dividend yield was 5.4% from a company that had approximately doubled in size in the previous decade. Its PE10 ratio was just 13, which is very low for such a rapidly growing company.

In the following months the share price rocketed up to 380p and I eventually sold at 359p. I pocketed a total gain of more than 50% in just eight months, which of course is probably more down to luck than skill.

Some investors say you should sell your losers and ride your winners, but in most cases I would completely disagree with that. I sold N Brown precisely because the shares were winners.

The share price increased by 50% and yet the company's revenues, earnings and dividends had essentially stayed the same. As a result of the rapid price increase the dividend yield dropped from 5.4% to 3.6% and the PE10 ratio increased from 13 to 20. While those valuation metrics were still good relative to other similarly successful companies, they weakened the company's defensive value rank to the point where it was one of the lowest ranked holdings in my portfolio.

Eventually, other companies that I didn't own started to be significantly more attractively valued than N Brown – in other words their defensive value rank was much better (numerically lower). So in January 2013 I sold the company, locked in those capital gains and the following month I reinvested the proceeds into one of those more attractively valued alternatives.

2. An underperforming company leads to weakening fundamental factors

Although I don't like to sell when things go wrong, sometimes it does make sense. If a company goes into a major slump, either rapidly or over a period of years, its growth rate and growth quality are likely to decline, and at some point the company may no longer be good enough to justify its position in your portfolio.

Selling Balfour Beatty after several years of declining results

A recent example of this in my case was Balfour Beatty, whose lacklustre results we've already looked at.

When I bought Balfour Beatty in August 2011 it had an attractive set of statistics. Its growth rate was 14.1%, its growth quality was 81% and its profitability was 17%. Those are all solid numbers and were much better than the market average.

Of course my hope for any investment is that it does well, but as we've seen that wasn't the case for Balfour. It struggled along under growing debts and pension obligations until 2014 when it fell off the proverbial cliff. The dividend was suspended and the company posted a significant loss.

As a result of that loss and the suspended dividend, its growth rate fell from 14.1% to -0.8%, breaking my minimum 2% rule. Growth quality also fell from 81.5% to 59.3% while profitability fell from 17.2% to 10.8%. One notable item that didn't fall was the debt ratio, which grew from 0.3 to 5.4 (and therefore beyond the maximum value of 4 for cyclical companies) as its borrowings ballooned from £48m to £472m.

You can see the impact of these changes on some of Balfour's various factors in Table 13.1.

	1 August 2011	1 April 2015
Price	254p	232p
Growth rate	14.1%	-0.8%
Growth quality	81.5%	59.3%
Profitability	17.2%	10.8%
PE10	12.1	10.2
Yield	4.8%	2.3%
Debt ratio	0.3	5.4

Table 13.1: Balfour Beatty's weakening fundamentals

Balfour went from having a record of fast and consistent growth, a strong balance sheet and a good dividend yield in 2011, to having none of those in 2015. Its growth rate and debt ratio also fell outside my acceptable ranges and as a result the stock no longer looked attractive.

I sold Balfour in April 2015, which was a designated sell month. I started the process as I usually do, by revaluing all of my existing holdings and then calculating their defensive value ranks. Table 13.2 shows my five lowest ranked holdings at the time, which is the group I'll typically make sell decisions from.

Rank	Company	Dividend yield	Growth rate	PE10
26	BP	5.7%	-0.5%	9.1
27	RSA Insurance	0.5%	-12.2%	8.5
28	BAE Systems	3.9%	2.8%	15.6

Rank	Company	Dividend yield	Growth rate	PE10
29	Serco Group	2.2%	-4.9%	14.1
30	Balfour Beatty	2.3%	-0.8%	10.2

Table 13.2: Balfour Beatty compared to several of my holdings in April 2015

For the most part this is not a group of outstanding success stories: BP had been under significant pressure since its Gulf of Mexico oil spill in 2010; RSA had recently cut its dividend and raised additional capital through a rights issue; Serco had suspended its dividend and completed a rights issue; and Balfour had faced its fair share of problems. Out of that group only BAE Systems, the UK's largest defence and manufacturing company, had been a relatively successful investment up to that point.

So there I was in April 2015, faced with a decision of what to sell. Should I sell BAE Systems and lock in significant profits (a capital gain of 70% at the time), or make a hard choice and pick one of the portfolio's underperformers? Without being able to see into the future there was – and is – no way to know which one was the right choice.

My preference is always to sell the weakest holding (Balfour in this case), unless there is a particularly good reason to sell something else. On top of that I'd rather lock in a profit than a loss, and Balfour was showing a small net profit at the time (i.e. its small capital loss had been more than offset by dividend income) while BP, RSA and Serco were showing losses, even with dividends included. But I didn't want to hold on to those losing shares forever, and holding on to shares just because they're showing a loss is a good way to hold on to underperforming companies. Another consideration was that I'd rather hold on to shares with a good yield (BP and possibly BAE) and get rid of those where the dividend had been suspended (Balfour and Serco).

So all of these different factors come into play, which is largely by design. In the end, some degree of personal judgment is required, and that's perfectly fine by me. In fact, I much prefer it that way, rather than simply ticking the boxes that my investment strategy tells me to tick.

In this case I decided to go with the default option of selling Balfour, partly because it was the lowest ranked stock, but also because of its suspended dividend and excessively high debt and pension ratios.

The decision to sell a company because of weakening fundamentals or high valuations can be combined under the following rule of thumb.

Defensive value rule of thumb

Choose which holding to sell from the five weakest holdings (according to whatever stock selection method you use). Don't just mechanically sell the weakest stock; take ownership of the decision by taking a number of factors into account as you see fit.

---

3. The company has become a value trap

Another reason to sell is when you think a company has become a value trap, or has a high probability of becoming one soon. Although your opinion on a company's value trap risk could change at any time, I typically leave making this judgment until after a holding publishes its latest annual results. I will then work through the value trap and competitive advantage questions as part of my yearly review task.

If anything has changed during the year that significantly undermines my previous opinion of the company then it could well affect my preference for holding onto it or getting rid of it.

Some of the quantitative indicators from the value trap questions that can be relevant here are:

1. **Large acquisitions** – If a company starts to spend significant amounts of money (more than the current year's post-tax profit) on acquisitions, especially if it does this in multiple years, it may be increasing the likelihood of trouble down the road.

2. **High and growing capex** – Increasing amounts of capital expenditure, especially if those amounts are already high (more than post-tax profits), can sometimes be a sign of a company struggling to grow, and perhaps over-investing in order to generate growth at any cost. Also watch for increasing debts, which may be used to fund this increase.

3. **Declining profitability** – This can sometimes go hand in hand with increasing capex. The company may be investing in low-return opportunities to grow earnings per share, but if these opportunities are generating relatively low rates of return on capital then they will destroy shareholder value rather than create it. It would be better for shareholders if that money had been returned to them as a dividend. I will normally look for declining profitability over the whole ten-year period for which I have data.

In many situations there will be no hard numbers to back up your belief that a company has become a potential value trap. The company may have launched into a major new project which has little to do with its core business, or perhaps its key market is being disrupted by new technology and it seems obvious that its current offering will be obsolete within a few years.

Whether or not the risk of a company turning into a value trap is too high is a difficult judgment to make, but I still feel it is worthwhile having an opinion about it. If I think the risks around a particular holding are too high then I will look to offload it sooner, but only once it becomes one of the portfolio's five weakest holdings.

Defensive value rule of thumb

Take the value trap and competitive advantage questions into account when making sell decisions.

---

4. The position has become too large

If an investment does exceptionally well it could grow to the point where it adversely affects the portfolio's diversity. As I hold 30 companies the default starting size for each holding is 3.3% (1/30th of the total), although in reality it tends to be somewhere between 3% and 4% depending on how much cash is available for reinvestment. When a holding gets close to more than twice the default size I start to become uncomfortable with it and so I sell around half of any holding which goes beyond that level in order to return it back to the default position size.

Defensive value rule of thumb

When a holding gets close to twice the default position size sell around half to return it to the default size.

I still restrict myself to making this rebalancing trade during the first week of the month, but I don't restrict it to sell months. If, for example, it was a buy month and one of my holdings had grown to 7% of the portfolio, I would still go ahead with the planned buy transaction, but I would also sell enough of that excessively large position to reduce it back to the 3% to 4% range (I'm not obsessed with reducing it exactly back to 3.3%).

The same would apply during a sell month. I would completely exit whichever holding appeared to offer the least attractive combination of features, and at the same time I would sell around half of any position that had grown too large.

The primary goal of this rebalancing exercise is to reduce risk by controlling the portfolio's exposure to any one company, but it is also an effective way to take profits on investments that have performed exceptionally well.

Rebalancing JD Sports after rapid share price gains

One company I have had to rebalance more than once is JD Sports, the high street sports fashion retailer.

I first bought shares in JD in March 2011 for 228p (adjusted for stock splits). After a couple of years in which the shares went nowhere they suddenly started to take off in mid-2013. By October 2014 the share price had increased to 435p, giving me a nice 91% capital gain in three and a half years.

However, because of those gains JD's position size had increased to 6.1% of my portfolio, which is large enough to start making me nervous, so I sold about half the shares to bring the investment back down towards the 3% to 4% range. The cash from that sale was then recycled back into another company at the next buy month. JD's share price continued to climb and just a few months later it once again made up a significant portion of the portfolio. When the shares reached 649p in June 2015 I sold around half of the position, for a second time, to bring the investment back down to an acceptable size.

You might say I would have been better off if I hadn't rebalanced at all and had, instead, just held the original investment for the full gain from 228p to 649p. That's true, but at the time it was in no way obvious that the shares would keep going up after I rebalanced them at 435p, or that they would keep going up after I rebalanced them at 649p. However, if I hadn't rebalanced, JD's position size would now be more than 12% of the portfolio which would represent a massive risk from a single company.

Personally I prefer to reduce risk by rebalancing rather than hanging on to an excessively large position in the hope that it keeps going up.

5. The dividend has been suspended for more than a year

One event that will automatically lead me to sell a company is if it fails to pay a dividend for an entire financial year. There are a couple of reasons for this.

First, I am willing to accept that in extreme circumstances a company may need to suspend its dividend, typically in order to strengthen its balance sheet. This usually indicates that the company has been badly run in some way, but usually a suspended dividend will result in the executive management team *being replaced*, and a new team being brought in to turn things around. I am willing to hold on through this turnaround period, even if it takes several years.

However, I would not expect the dividend to be suspended across an entire financial year. I would expect any company with a competitive core business to be able to restore some semblance of stability and profitability, and therefore its dividend, within a relatively short period of time.

Second, and more practically, a zero dividend will mean that the company fails my ten-year unbroken record of dividend payments rule of thumb. It will also severely mess up the calculations for several of the defensive value factors, most notably the growth rate. I could design a workaround for this but since I don't like companies that suspend the dividend for extended periods anyway, I am comfortable selling automatically if the dividend for an entire financial year falls to zero.

This may sound drastic, but in the last five years I have not had to do this once.

Defensive value rule of thumb

Sell a company if the dividend for the latest financial year falls to zero.

Deciding what not to sell

In Chapter 12 we looked at various situations in which selling may not be the best idea in the world, such as selling on news of a profit warning, dividend cut or rights issue. Here I'll look at a slightly different situation, where I deliberately avoid selling the lowest ranked (weakest) holding for some reason, and instead sell a higher ranked (less weak) holding, although still one of the bottom five.

I have already mentioned that selling can involve considerations other than the defensive value factors and how a holding performs on your stock selection system. You might decide, for example, to hold onto the weakest stock in your portfolio because you believe it is capable of high rates of growth over the next few years, perhaps because of an impressively successful international expansion program. This is a subjective decision but I think as long as you stick within the general principle of selling less attractive holdings then this sort of flexibility is useful and makes the whole investing process more interesting.

In my case I don't like to sell holdings that are significantly out of favour with other investors. I am a contrarian by nature and so I prefer to buy on bad news and sell on good news. Also, I don't like to sell at a loss if I think there is a chance I can avoid it. That may sound speculative, and it is, but as I've said I like to leave some wiggle room in the decision-making process so that it isn't entirely mechanical and so that I can give my foibles some breathing space, no matter how irrational.

A recent example of this aversion to selling on bad news or selling at a loss is RSA Group, the leading but recently struggling insurance company.

Escaping from the RSA value trap thanks to a bit of patience and a lot of luck

When I bought RSA in early 2012 I was still in the early stages of developing the defensive value investing approach. I didn't have any real idea of how to assess the riskiness of an insurance company, and eventually that lack of knowledge came back to bite me.

In simple terms RSA had been struggling since the turn of the millennium from a mixture of weak profitability, excessive investment in the stock market and excessive leverage (i.e. its premium to surplus ratio was too high). However, I did not really understand that at the time. I thought that any bad news was already in the price as the dividend yield at the time of purchase was 8.8% – a red flag if ever there was one.

Clearly the market expected that dividend to be cut, and in early 2013 it was. As you know, I don't sell on dividend cuts, so I held on, but the news didn't get any better. In late 2013 after some irregularities in its Ireland business, the CEO resigned and eventually the dividend was suspended and a rights issue was announced. From that description of events it should be obvious that RSA was a value trap and I had completely missed the warning signs.

After the 2013 results were published in February 2014, RSA's growth rate turned negative and it became one of the lowest (worst) ranked holdings according to its defensive value rank. In April 2014 it actually was the lowest ranked holding, but I sold Mears Group instead. Why? Because it seemed that everyone hated RSA so my contrarian nature made me want to hold on, and selling would also have locked in a significant capital loss. Mears, on the other hand, was in favour with investors and the investment had produced an annualised return of 25%, which I was keen to lock in.

Two months later I sold AstraZeneca for an almost 17% annualised return, even though RSA was once again ranked lower. The story was the same: AstraZeneca had done well, its valuation was no longer attractive and I wanted to lock in the gains. RSA in contrast had done badly; it was still showing a loss and I hoped that the company could be turned around, or at least give the appearance that it was being turned around, to the point where the market and share price would respond positively.

Another two months after that (August 2014) I sold Royal Dutch Shell for a 31% annualised return and the situation was very similar. Shell was in favour and showing a fantastic return while RSA was the opposite. They were both in the bottom five of my holdings according to their defensive value rank and so I chose to lock in the profits from Shell.

In October 2014 I sold Greggs (the baker) for a 15% annualised return and in December I sold Imperial Tobacco for a 17% annualised return, and yet still in both cases RSA had a lower rank. I was holding on for some good news from RSA, although through this period I questioned the sanity of this decision many times.

Before you start thinking I'm a blind optimist who refuses to sell anything at a loss, that's not quite true. In mid-2015 I was faced with a small collection of underperformers and if I had resolutely avoided selling any of them I would have had to sell some much better stocks instead, which is something I didn't want to do. Instead I sold Balfour in April 2015 for a paltry 3% annualised return and in June of that year I sold Serco for a 50% capital loss. Both had performed badly, both were among the bottom five ranked holdings and both were surrounded by bad news. I decided to sell Balfour and Serco rather than RSA because I thought (or perhaps felt) that both companies had poor prospects for a short-term turnaround, while RSA's prospects seemed better.

Again, I will point out that these speculations about short-term future prospects are just that – my personal speculations. I don't think they have any particularly strong basis in fact, but they allow me to exercise some judgment and, as long as I stick to the basic system of selling from the bottom five ranked stocks, I don't think such speculation can do too much damage.

Eventually I did manage to sell RSA at a profit, albeit a small one. Thanks to a takeover offer from Zurich Insurance in July 2015, the share price spiked up by about 20% in one day and shortly after I was able to sell the stock for a 6% annualised gain. Shortly after that the takeover offer was withdrawn and the shares collapsed to where they had been before.

Whether this happy outcome was primarily down to luck (which it obviously was to some extent – I had no idea a takeover offer was imminent), or whether my speculations about RSA's ability to turn itself around were in fact grounded in some of the knowledge I've built up over the years, there is no way to tell for sure.

However, the investment did work out well in the end and so on that basis I am happy to continue to hold where a combination of bad news and paper losses make a sale unattractive, and where I think there is a good chance the situation will improve sooner rather than later.

In the next chapter I'll turn to the topic of continuous improvement through continuous learning, and the need to learn from both good investments and bad.

As a summary though, here are those selling rules of thumb once more.

Rules of thumb for selling deliberately

- Alternate buying or selling one holding each month.

- Choose which holding to sell from the five weakest holdings (according to whatever stock selection method you use). Don't just mechanically sell the lowest ranked stock; take ownership of the decision by taking a number of factors into account as you see fit.

- Take the value trap and competitive advantage questions into account when making sell decisions.

- When a holding gets close to twice the default position size sell around half to return it to the default size.

- Sell a company if the dividend for the latest financial year falls to zero.

CHAPTER 14.

Improve Continuously

> *"When we think about what we are doing in terms of learning and mastering, accepting that we may make some mistakes along the way, we stay motivated despite the setbacks that might occur."*
>
> HEIDI GRANT HALVORSON, AUTHOR OF *NINE THINGS SUCCESSFUL PEOPLE DO DIFFERENTLY*

There is no such thing as perfection in the world of investing. Every investment strategy can be improved and every investor can enhance their knowledge and skills as the world around them evolves in unexpected ways.

For me this is one of the great joys of investing. There is always something to learn, some new way to look at the world or some existing knowledge to be applied with greater skill.

Even Warren Buffett was not born as one of the world's great investors. He reached the top only after many years of continuously improving his skills and knowledge, by absorbing lessons wherever he could find them, even if that meant going to Columbia University to study under (and eventually work for) his investment idol, Benjamin Graham.

In much the same way the investment strategy in this book did not simply pop into my head, fully formed, one sunny afternoon. It is the accumulation of many lessons learned over many years. While each individual lesson may seem small and perhaps unimportant, when compounded they should make an enormous difference to the effectiveness of the strategy over a multi-decade period.

In this chapter I'll outline how I go about improving the investment strategy in a consistent and deliberate manner.

Standing on the shoulders of giants

Knowledge is the foundation upon which all future improvement and learning is based and one of the most effective ways to expand your knowledge is to learn from others. The logic of this is simple: I know that there are many other investors who are smarter, harder working and far more experienced than I am. It would be foolish of me not to take advantage of that fact, learn from their successes and mistakes and make use of those lessons where possible.

For me this usually means a regular diet of reading books and articles and watching videos. I'm not obsessive about this though and I probably don't get anywhere near the figure of 500 pages a day which Warren Buffett apparently reads. I would say I read a few articles each day and perhaps a book every month or two. That isn't supposed to be some optimal amount; it's just what works for me.

The point is that you read at least something new and informative on a regular basis so that you build up a store of knowledge which you can then draw upon at some point down the road.

If I had to suggest a reading list to a new value investor it would probably look something like this:

- *The New Buffettology* by Mary Buffett

- *Warren Buffett and the Interpretation of Financial Statements* by Mary Buffett
- *The Intelligent Investor* by Benjamin Graham
- *The Most Important Thing* by Howard Marks
- *The Intelligent Asset Allocator* by William Bernstein
- *Irrational Exuberance* by Robert Shiller
- *Valuing Wall Street* by Andrew Smithers

These books cover investing from a variety of angles, from psychology to picking individual stocks, portfolio construction and market-wide factors. I think that as a group they're probably as good a set of books to get started with as any.

Having said all that, it's also important that you don't throw out your existing investment strategy every time you find something new and exciting. I am a firm believer in evolutionary rather than revolutionary improvements, so once you've found a strategy that works for you, you should be looking to stick with it and incrementally improve it over many years.

Learning from your mistakes

As important as reading is, I think the most significant lessons will come from your own experiences as an investor. It is one thing to read about reducing position sizes to reduce risk, but quite another to see a significant portion of your portfolio destroyed because of overexposure to a single company.

So when an investment goes wrong and you make a loss, don't run for the exit and attempt to banish the mistake from your memory; use it as an opportunity to learn and improve. Do your best to understand why you made the mistake, or if it wasn't a mistake, find out why the investment turned out badly. The knowledge that you gain from this analysis, if applied intelligently to your strategy in the future, could well lead to additional gains that are far beyond what you could ever have achieved if the original investment had turned out well.

For this reason I prefer to think of the full investment lifecycle of each holding not as buy-hold-sell, but as buy-hold-sell-improve. This means that selling is not the final chapter for each individual investment (or for this book). Instead, I always perform a post-mortem after every sell decision.

If something particularly bad happens to an investment then it may be possible to learn valuable lessons and make important improvements even before it has been sold. In situations where things are going from bad to worse I tend to ask questions like:

1. Why did the problem occur?

2. Was it obvious the problem was coming?

3. Could I have avoided this investment without overly restricting the universe of stocks I'm happy to invest in?

4. Is there a metric (either an existing one or one I can invent) that I can use to look for this problem in future?

5. Is there a pattern between this problem and similar problems in other companies?

As I've already mentioned, I don't immediately sell an investment when something goes wrong. This willingness to stay with a problematic holding enables me to calmly review the situation and try to get something positive out of it. The goal, of course, is to try to avoid the same problem in future but without reducing returns by being overly cautious.

If I do find something like a ratio or a question that can act as a warning flag, I may add it into my selection criteria. However, it's important not to restrict the stock selection criteria to the point where virtually no company is deemed to be safe enough.

You might, for example, invest in a company which subsequently cuts its dividend. You might come to the conclusion that the dividend was cut because the company was generating an insufficient amount of free cash flow (cash from operations minus interest, taxes and capital expenses). To fix the problem you might insist that all future investments have a free cash flow to dividend ratio of 2, i.e. the company's free cash flow should be twice as large as its dividend.

This may well reduce the number of dividend cuts that you see, but it might also mean you don't invest in lots of perfectly good companies that just happen to fail this fairly strict test. The risk is that you miss out on good companies that would in fact have produced excellent returns over many years.

So there is a trade-off between reducing risk by increasing the strictness of your investment criteria, and reducing returns by reducing the number of companies (including good ones) that meet those criteria.

That's why I take an evolutionary rather than revolutionary approach to improving my strategy. If something happens which indicates a weakness in the strategy then I'll make a small change rather than a big change. I can then run the strategy with the small change for a number of months or even years, in order to gain more experience with the latest tweaks. If the same problem occurs again then I can make another small change, but if not then the small change may have worked, and hopefully without making the investment strategy too risk averse.

As you might expect, I have a rule of thumb for this process.

Defensive value rule of thumb

If an investment runs into serious problems try to understand the root causes as soon as possible so that the investment strategy can be improved and similar problems avoided in future.

Perform a post-sale review of every investment in order to learn as much as possible and potentially improve the strategy for future investments.

I think it's time we looked at some examples from my own extensive list of mistakes.

Overpaying for Chemring leads to a more cautious approach to valuing companies

Chemring Group is a small-cap company operating in the Aerospace & Defensive sector. It is one of the world's leading developers of technologies that detect and counter a variety of threats, including improvised explosive devices, biological agents and guided missiles.

I first invested in Chemring in 2011 and at the time the company had a spectacular history of rapid and consistent growth, with a growth rate of over 31% and growth quality of 85%. However, I certainly paid full price for that track record. With a share price of 689p the PE10 ratio was over 40 while the PD10 ratio was sky high at more than 150. With a dividend of 11.8p per share the yield was also a less than spectacular 1.7%.

Those ratios are way outside my current rules of thumb, so why did I invest at such a lofty price?

The answer is that at the time I didn't have those rules of thumb. In fact I used a completely different system for valuing companies based on a ratio I'd dreamed up called PEGY10, which was calculated as:

PEGY10 = PE10 / (growth rate + yield)

This is an extension of the PEGY ratio, which may have been devised by Peter Lynch, a famous American investor. The idea is to compare a company's valuation multiple (PE10 in the case of PEGY10) against its expected rate of return, i.e. the yield plus the growth rate.

PEGY10 worked well for a while, but Chemring highlighted a problem with it. If a company had an extremely high growth rate then even an extremely high valuation could appear to be justified. With Chemring at 689p the ratio was:

PEGY10 = 40.7 / (31.7 + 1.7) = 1.2

Anything close to or below 1 was extremely cheap and so with a PEGY10 ratio of 1.2 Chemring appeared to be attractively priced.

But what happens if that high growth rate is not sustained?

Let's imagine that after I'd invested, Chemring's growth rate fell from 31.7% to 10% (a still respectable rate of growth) over a period of several years, while everything else stayed the same, including the share price. In that case the PEGY10 ratio would climb to 3.5, which is high. The implication would be that Chemring was now expensive, even though the share price is the same as it was before. The only thing that happened was that the exceptionally high historic growth rate had not been maintained.

The risk here is that as the company's growth rate drops the market might decide that the shares are no longer worthy of such a high valuation multiple. If the PEGY10 ratio fell back to its previously attractive level of 1.2, but with the company's growth rate now at 10% instead of 31.7%, the share price would have to drop by about 60%.

By accepting a PE10 ratio of more than 40 I was leaving myself open to a massive share price decline if the future did not turn out to be as rosy as the past, and that's exactly what happened. Chemring's results after 2011 nosedived, the shares did indeed fall by more than 60% and they have yet to recover.

This led me to search for a new approach to valuation. One still based around ten-year results and the PE10 ratio, but where a company with twice the growth rate of another company would not be worth twice the PE10 ratio, which is what the PEGY10 ratio implied.

The result of my research was the defensive value rank detailed in Chapter 6, where each factor is ranked independently of the others. This means that a company with twice the growth rate of another company is worthy of higher valuation multiples, but nowhere near twice as high. This ranking approach has proven itself to be far more robust than the PEGY10 ratio, which is why I still use it today.

As an additional sanity check I also introduced the PE10 rule of thumb, where I will almost never invest if the ratio is above 30. This helps me to avoid overpaying for a company, no matter how good its track record.

Operational problems with Chemring leads to the avoidance of heavily acquisitive companies

Another valuable lesson I learned from Chemring was the danger of companies that grow by borrowing to acquire other companies. When I reviewed and purchased Chemring in early 2011 I knew that the company had grown by acquisition, but I did not realise how problematic this could be.

After seeing the company's revenues, profits and dividends fall in 2012, 2013 and 2014, I reviewed the company again in order to avoid making the same mistake. I came to the conclusion that a debt-fuelled acquisition strategy was at the root of the company's problems and that with the proper tools, this value trap could have been avoided.

I spent some time analysing the acquisition histories of many different companies, where some had gotten into trouble and some hadn't. Eventually I settled on my current approach to acquisitions which is detailed in Chapter 7. Just as a reminder, the approach is to be wary of (or even avoid) companies that have either frequently spent more on acquisitions in a single year than they earned in that year, or where they have spent more on acquisitions in the last ten years than they earned in those ten years.

In Chemring's case it spent more on acquisitions than it earned in profit in seven out of the previous ten years: in 2001, 2005 to 2009 and 2010. In total it spent more than 140% of its normalised post-tax profits on acquisitions over that whole period. Under the current rules this would have been more than enough reason to avoid Chemring.

As well as making many large acquisitions, the majority of those acquisitions were paid for with borrowed money. Borrowings went from £43m to £365m in just a few years, taking the debt ratio to more than 7 and well outside my maximum of 5. Unfortunately I didn't use the debt ratio at the time and the measure I was using – interest cover – didn't flag Chemring as being over-indebted.

Eventually I did introduce the debt ratio and I gradually made it more conservative thanks to other problematic investments. If I had been using it in 2011 it would have been another indicator, along with the history of large acquisitions, that Chemring was an investment to avoid.

Dividend cuts at Aviva and RSA lead to improvements in the insurance company metrics

When I bought these two large-cap insurance companies I only had the most basic ideas about how to analyse insurance companies. That didn't put me off from investing because I believe in learning by experience, so I'm happy to invest a small amount into unfamiliar situations in order to learn. In this case both investments ran into considerable trouble, but as a result of that trouble I learned a great deal and (thanks to some luck) managed to achieve a reasonable return on each of them.

The basic problem for both Aviva and RSA was a combination of weak profitability from their insurance businesses and insufficient capital relative to the amount of insurance they were writing. While I owned their shares these problems led to dividend cuts for each company and a rights issue for RSA. This is not good of course and so I decided to find out why my investment strategy hadn't seen these events coming.

My mistake wasn't that I hadn't looked at profitability or capital ratios at all, because I did. But at the time I had weaker or non-existent rules of thumb.

On the profitability side I looked at the company's combined ratio for the current year, but was only really interested in it being below 100% (i.e. their underwriting businesses were barely profitable), and even that wasn't a rule of thumb. For both companies the ratio was below 100%, but only just.

On the capital side I thought the official EU Insurance Group Directive (IGD) capital requirements would be a good place to start, so my initial rule of thumb was that insurance companies should have surplus capital beyond that required by the IGD.

However, hindsight makes it clear that the official capital requirements are woefully inadequate if you want the insurance companies you invest in to avoid dividend cuts and rights issues.

In 2014 I decided that I needed a better set of rules for analysing insurance companies. After a fair amount of reading, thinking and spreadsheet fiddling, I came up with much stiffer rules on profitability (Chapter 3) and capital (Chapter 4). My expectation now is that these rules will remain largely unchanged for at least a few years while my experience with insurance companies grows.

If every insurance company I invest in from now on works out well then the rules will remain unchanged. If different problems arise then I will learn from those problems and make additional changes to the strategy if necessary. If the same problems occur again then I may end up tightening the rules further, or replacing them with something else that will hopefully be more effective at spotting problematic companies.

The goal as always will be to invest, to learn and to improve.

A crisis at Tesco leads to a new focus on profitability

Another holding of mine which has run into problems is Tesco. When I purchased the company's shares in June 2012 it was still flying high, with a long record of extremely impressive growth. Warren Buffett had recently increased his stake in the company, which is about as good an endorsement as you can get. However, in mid-2014, after a series of profit warnings, the CEO left and that was followed shortly after by a major accounting scandal, where the company's profits had been overstated by more than £250m.

Given that Tesco operates in the defensive Food & Drug Retailer sector and is the epitome of a defensive stock for most people, I was not expecting it to be a value trap, but that's exactly what it turned out to be. Clearly there was more going wrong than just a £250m profit overstatement, as the company's revenues, profits and dividends were in freefall, to the point where the dividend was suspended in 2015.

One issue that reared its head again was debt. Tesco's problems, along with problems at other companies I owned such as Morrisons, Serco and Balfour Beatty, showed that the debt ratio I was using at the time was too generous. So in early 2015 I changed the way it was calculated (to the method detailed in Chapter 4) and introduced the even tighter rules for cyclical sector companies. With the current more restrictive debt ratio I wouldn't have bought any of those companies. However, what I really want to talk about is the profitability score.

Back in 2012 I didn't use any measure of profitability, either to rank stocks or to rule them in or out as investment candidates. I'm not sure why, but I think it was because I had read that Buffett's preferred measure was Return on Equity (ROE) and, having analysed that ratio for hundreds of companies, I felt it was not robust enough to be usable. It could range from anywhere over 1000% to less than 0%, and the correlation between the quality of a company and its ROE was often weak. So instead of using ROE I simply did without a ratio for profitability altogether.

What got me thinking about profitability again was an article in the *Financial Times* by Terry Smith, a well-known City figure and fund manager. Smith's opinion was that Tesco's problems were predictable given a long running decline in its Return on Capital Employed (ROCE) figure. His article showed a chart of Tesco's earnings per share going from less than 10p in 1998 to more than 30p in 2011, while at the same time its ROCE declined from 19% to 14%. He even quoted Warren Buffett from 1979:

> "The primary test of managerial economic performance is the achievement of a high earnings rate on equity capital employed (without undue leverage, accounting gimmickry,

etc) and not the achievement of consistent gains in earnings per share."

I wouldn't say I had sleepless nights but Smith's article did keep popping into my head for several days. Eventually I realised that it probably was a mistake to analyse companies without taking account of their profitability.

Given that I didn't like ROE and that Smith had written about ROCE, I decided to investigate that ratio instead. I read some of Buffett's letter's to Berkshire Hathaway shareholders and re-read sections of several books including *The New Buffettology* by Mary Buffett and *Accounts Demystified* by Anthony Rice.

After running some tests using ROCE for hundreds of companies (using a spreadsheet and data from ShareScope), I found the ratio to be much less variable than ROE, ranging between 0% and 100% in almost all cases. A high ROCE, especially when averaged over several years, also seemed to be closely correlated with companies that required very little in the way of capital expenditure. That was an added bonus because high capex companies are often seen as more risky, especially when inflation is high. And so after some additional head scratching I devised the profitability score laid out in Chapter 3.

Although Tesco's ten-year median net ROCE (i.e. its profitability) was not so low as to make it uninvestible, including the profitability score in the valuation process back in 2012 may well have led to me not investing in the company at all. Tesco's relatively low profitability (below 10%) would have been a negative factor in its defensive value rank calculation, meaning a lower share price than the one I actually paid in 2012 would have been required in order for the shares to be attractive.

The share price continued to decline through 2014 and so at some point the price and valuation ratios may have been low enough that the shares looked attractive, even given the company's low profitability. However, by that point Tesco's other problems would have become so obvious that I probably wouldn't have wanted to invest anyway. And even if I had invested in 2014 rather than 2012, it would have been at a significantly lower share price and therefore the (paper) loss the investment is currently showing would have been much smaller.

From those examples it may look as if virtually every investment goes wrong or runs into significant problems, but that is very far from the truth. In my experience over the past five years as a defensive value investor there have been many more successes than failures, and I expect that trend to continue. So let's have a look at what lessons we can learn from that more positive side of investing.

Learning from your successes

Successful investments, while very satisfying, generally provide fewer valuable lessons than unsuccessful investments. When I sell a company's shares after a multi-year period in which that company consistently grew its revenues, earnings and dividends, the main lesson is a sort of confirmation that my selection criteria worked. In other words, the criteria correctly selected a successful company which continued to be successful over a long enough period for me to profit from it in a meaningful way.

I would say that the lessons from successful investments are less likely to come from individual events or companies, and more likely to come as a result of many similar types of investment performing well.

For example, you might find that those companies with the highest growth quality and profitability tend to be the best investments, regardless of price. Or, you may find that the shares bought on the lowest valuation ratios perform best, and that growth and quality are less important. In either case you might decide to focus on investing in the types of stocks that do best, whilst still maintaining the broad portfolio diversity which is so important.

Unfortunately I do not have much to say on this issue as I have yet to see a significant outperformance by one particular type of defensive value stock. Perhaps that will be something to cover in the second edition of this book.

Even less educational are those investments where the success was primarily due to a rapid and short-term increase in the share price. If you invest in a company's shares at 100p and within a year they're at 200p, it's unlikely that you'll be able to learn anything from that investment which you can apply repeatedly to future investments.

You may uncover the reason for the increase, but it is very likely to be company-specific and not applicable to other companies. More generally, I think that trying to predict which shares will see rapid short-term price gains is like trying to predict the role of a dice or next week's lottery numbers; virtually impossible and generally a waste of time.

Learning from the world around you

There are lessons to be found everywhere, whether in books, academic papers, websites, conversations with people, hobbies, sport, or life in general.

For example, by reading about stoic philosophy I learned the importance of concentrating on what you can control rather than what you cannot control. This is a helpful way to look at investing, where most of the short and medium-term results are out of your control, as are the results of any company you invest in. It's only by focusing on what you can control – which is your personal decisions and actions driven by your knowledge and investment strategy – that you can achieve long-term success as an investor.

Now that we have covered the very last step in the investment process, all that remains for me to do is list the rules of thumb covered in this chapter.

Rules of thumb for improving continuously

- If an investment runs into serious problems try to understand the root causes as soon as possible so that the investment strategy can be improved and similar problems avoided in future.

- Perform a post-sale review of every investment in order to learn as much as possible and potentially improve the strategy for future investments.

APPENDIX

Free resources

The investment approach laid out in this book involves a fair number of calculations and in many places I have mentioned the benefits of having a spreadsheet which is set up to do the calculations for you.

If you're not keen on developing your own spreadsheet you are more than welcome to download some readymade ones from my website. The spreadsheets may change over time, but currently they include the following:

1. **Company Analysis Spreadsheets** – Automatically calculates all of the defensive value factors such as growth rate, growth quality and so on for a given company.

2. **Portfolio Analysis Spreadsheet** – Calculates a portfolio's geographic, size and sector diversity. Will also calculate the defensive value rank for a list of stocks.

3. **Company Analysis Questions** – Not a spreadsheet, but a document containing all of the value trap and competitive advantage questions with space for your answers.

There are also printable worksheets if you don't like spreadsheets. You can download these for free at: www.ukvalueinvestor.com/free-resources

Data providers supplying ten years of data

Here is a summary of the main data providers I use on a regular basis.

ShareScope and SharePad

At the moment I get most of my data from ShareScope and SharePad, and they're the systems I refer back to most often.

ShareScope (www.sharescope.co.uk) is a downloadable desktop program with a huge amount of functionality. It gives me the ten years of data for each company that I'm after and the ability to track the value of real or virtual portfolios.

SharePad (www.sharepad.co.uk) is the online version of ShareScope, although it is somewhat simpler and aimed more at investors rather than traders (ShareScope has a lot of elaborate charting functionality which is only of interest to traders). SharePad has the ten years of data I want and gives a nice breakdown of the income statements, balance sheets and cash flow statements for each year, which makes it easy to enter that data into a spreadsheet.

Morningstar Premium

Morningstar Premium (www.morningstar.co.uk) shows up to ten years of financial data on a single page. If you don't want to pay for the Premium package then Morningstar provides five years of data for free.

Sharelockholmes

Sharelockholmes (sharelockholmes.com) is another website that has ten years of data for each company on a single screen. It is more basic than ShareScope or SharePad, but it's also cheaper and still has almost all the data you'll need to use this investment strategy.

Company websites

Most listed companies have a corporate website which includes a section for investors. Somewhere on the investor relations website or webpage you'll find an archive of annual results and reports. The annual, interim and quarterly results are typically available as downloadable press releases while the annual report is usually much more detailed and full of graphics and pictures. You can also usually find other news and announcements from the Regulatory News Service (RNS).

Many of these corporate websites won't have results and reports going back ten years, but they're still a good place to start.

FE Investegate

FE Investegate (www.investegate.co.uk) is my preferred place to search for official announcements from the Regulatory News Service (RNS).

It has all the official and regulatory news, including annual and interim results, interim (quarterly) management statements and other must-know pieces of information going back over many years.

The site is not entirely intuitive, but it only takes a few visits to work out where the information you need is located. You can also subscribe to new updates for individual companies via RSS

(Really Simple Syndication), which is how I keep up to date with the companies I'm invested in.

FTSE 100 revenues, earnings & dividends data

In Chapter 6 I talked about various methods for deciding whether a stock is a potential candidate for further analysis and investment. Some of the methods, including my defensive value rank method, need the defensive value factors to be calculated for the overall market, e.g. the FTSE 100. This means we need ten years of financial data for the FTSE 100. You can see the data for the ten years to 2015 in Table A.1.

Year	2006	2007	2008	2009	2010	2011	2012	2013	2014	2015
Revenues (m)	1,910	2,020	1,970	1,790	1,770	2,070	2,240	2,320	2,330	2,490
Earnings	477	546	500	304	486	554	523	487	433	360
Dividends	191	202	197	179	177	207	224	232	233	249

Table A.1: FTSE 100 financial results (in index points) for the ten years to the end of 2015

I have converted those figures into the defensive value factors using an example value for the FTSE 100 of 7000, which you can see in Table A.2.

Factor	FTSE 100
Example index price	7000
Growth rate	1.2%
Growth quality	55.6%
Profitability (estimated)	10.0%
PE10	15.0
PD10	33.5

Table A.2: Defensive value factors for the FTSE 100

Financial Times data archive

To calculate an index's earnings and dividends you'll need the index's price, PE ratio and dividend yield at a particular date (I use the last day of the year to calculate the annual figures for the FTSE 100). You can find index price, PE ratio and dividend yield data for the FTSE 100 and other indices in the FT website's data archive (markets.ft.com/research/Markets/Data-Archive).

Performance

Although I've mentioned the performance of several of my investments, I haven't given you any idea of how an entire portfolio might perform if it was managed according to this strategy, so that's what I'll cover here.

Since 2011, when I first started investing in defensive value rather than deep value stocks, I have managed a virtual model portfolio alongside my real portfolio. This portfolio has bought and sold exactly the same stocks, at the same prices, as my real portfolio. The only difference is that the model portfolio doesn't have any inflows or outflows of cash, so its performance is easier to track.

I compare the model portfolio against another virtual portfolio which is invested solely in the Aberdeen UK Tracker Trust, which tracks the FTSE All-Share. Each portfolio started with a virtual £50,000 in March 2011 and each transaction includes stamp duty at 0.5% and broker commission at £10. All dividends are reinvested.

One important point is that, at the time of this book's publication, the track record of these portfolios only stretches back about five years, which is the absolute minimum period over which you should compare performance.

The model portfolio has three basic performance goals:

1. To produce higher total returns than the market
2. To have a higher dividend yield than the market, and
3. To be less risky or volatile than the market.

1. Higher total returns

So far the model portfolio has achieved its goal of beating the market on a total return basis, as Table A.3 shows. The level of outperformance to date is around 4% on an annualised basis, which is slightly more than I hoped for (I thought it would be possible to beat the market by about 3% a year over the long term).

However, as I pointed out above, the comparison period is quite short, so we shall have to wait to see if that gap gets significantly larger or smaller.

	Model portfolio (A)	FTSE All-Share tracker (B)	Difference (A) – (B)
Starting value	£50,000	£50,000	£0
2011 (from 01/03/11)	-6.9%	-3.4%	-3.5%
2012	20.4%	13.9%	6.5%
2013	25.8%	19.5%	6.3%
2014	1.2%	2.7%	-1.5%
2015 (to 01/11/15)	13.1%	1.0%	12.2%
Total return	61.5%	36.3%	25.2%
Annualised return	10.8%	6.9%	3.9%
Current value	£80,731	£68,162	£12,579

Table A.3: Total return per calendar year to November 2015

2. Higher dividend yield

The dividend yield on the model portfolio has at all times been higher than the yield on the FTSE All-Share tracker. The average yield has been 4.2% and 3.3% for the two portfolios, respectively. Table A.4 shows the annual dividend received (and reinvested) so far.

	Model portfolio (A)	FTSE All-Share tracker (B)	Difference (A) – (B)
2011 (from 01/03/11)	£825	£1,531	-£706
2012	£2,599	£1,742	£857
2013	£2,673	£1,937	£736
2014	£3,309	£2,769	£540
2015 (to 01/11/15)	£2,941	£2,384	£557
Total dividends	£12,374	£10,363	£1,984

Table A.4: Dividends reinvested per calendar year to November 2015

3. Lower risk

My preferred measure of risk is the maximum peak-to-trough decline over the past five years. I think this captures what most people mean by risk more effectively than purely volatility-based measures.

Since March 2011 the model portfolio has seen a maximum peak-to-trough decline of 8%, between July 2011 and January 2012. The FTSE All-Share tracker on the other hand suffered a maximum decline of 13.5% between June 2011 and October 2011. However, this is a slightly unfair comparison as the model portfolio was still in the *build-up* phase and still had a very significant cash position at that time, which of course reduces volatility.

Looking at the maximum declines from the start of 2012, where both portfolios were more or less fully invested, the maximum declines are 5.7% for the model portfolio (between April 2012 and June 2012) and 10.7% for the All-Share tracker (between June 2015 and October 2015). So even when fully invested in a selection of 30 stocks the model portfolio has still seen significantly less downside risk than the UK market index.

Individual investment returns

I think it is vital that investors focus primarily on the performance of their overall portfolio rather than the ups and downs of their individual holdings. An excessive focus on individual holdings and the inevitable losses which they will occasionally incur can drive even the hardiest investor out of the market and into cash, usually at precisely the wrong moment.

However, individual investment results do matter. To give you an idea of the range of returns that this investment strategy has produced, Table A.5 shows the returns from every completed investment (i.e. bought, held and then sold) that the model portfolio has seen between March 2011 and December 2015.

Company	Sold	Period held	Total return
Robert Wiseman Dairies (RWD)	Jan 2012	9 months	25%
UTV Media (UTV)	Jul 2012	7 months	45%
UK Mail Group (UKM)	Oct 2012	1 year	34%
Brown (N) Group (BWNG)	Jan 2013	8 months	50%
Reckitt Benckiser Group (RB.)	Apr 2013	2 years	47%
Interserve (IRV)	Jul 2013	2 years, 4 months	117%
Go-Ahead Group (GOG)	Oct 2013	1 year, 8 months	36%

Company	Sold	Period held	Total return
Aviva (AV.)	Jan 2014	1 year, 9 months	32%
Mears Group (MER)	Apr 2014	3 years	89%
AstraZeneca (AZN)	Jun 2014	3 years	55%
Royal Dutch Shell (RDSB)	Aug 2014	8 months	18%
Greggs (GRG)	Oct 2014	1 year, 10 months	30%
Imperial Tobacco Group (IMT)	Dec 2014	1 year, 9 months	28%
ICAP (IAP)	Feb 2015	2 years, 10 months	42%
Balfour Beatty (BBY)	Apr 2015	3 years, 8 months	9%
Serco Group (SRP)	Jun 2015	1 year, 1 month	-50%
RSA Insurance Group (RSA)	Aug 2015	3 years, 6 months	19%
Cranswick Group (CHG)	Oct 2015	2 years, 11 months	135%
JD Sports Fashion (JD.)	Dec 2015	4 years, 9 months	234%

Table A.5: Completed investment returns for the model portfolio to November 2015

As the table shows, I focused purely on buying stocks during the first year (there are no sales in 2011) and I didn't begin the process of regularly selling the weakest holding until July 2012

(Robert Wiseman Dairies was sold in January 2012 as the result of a takeover). Even then I only sold one company every three months.

Once I did start to replace the weakest holding on a regular basis the initial monthly buying and selling pattern was buy/buy/sell, i.e. two purchases for every one sale, as I continued to focus on increasing the number of holdings to 30. Once the portfolio reached 30 holdings I switched over to the alternating monthly buy/sell pattern detailed in Chapter 11, which continues today.

RULES OF THUMB CHECKLIST

- Only invest in a company if its ten-year dividend cover is greater than 1.

- Only invest in a company if its growth quality is above 50%.

- Only invest in a company if its growth rate is above 2%.

- Only invest in a company if its profitability is above 7%.

- Only invest in an insurance company if its five-year average combined ratio is less than 95%.

- Only invest in a cyclical company if its debt ratio is below 4.

- Only invest in a defensive company if its debt ratio is below 5.

- Only invest in a bank if its five-year average common equity tier 1 ratio is above 12%.

- Only invest in an insurance company if its five-year average premium to surplus ratio is less than 2.

- Only invest in a company if its pension ratio is less than 10.

- Only invest in a company if its combined debt and pension ratio is below 10.

- Only invest in a company if its PE10 ratio is below 30.

- Only invest in a company if its PD10 ratio is below 60.

- Only invest in a company if it meets a sufficient number of your pre-defined criteria.

- Only invest in a company if its defensive value rank is better (i.e. numerically lower) than that of the market index.

- Only invest in a company if its defensive value rank is better (i.e. numerically lower) than most of your existing holdings.

- Only invest if you are reasonably confident that the company is not a value trap.

- Prefer companies that have durable competitive advantages to those that have short-term advantages or no advantages.

- Prefer companies that have low-cost competitive advantages to those with advantages that are expensive to maintain.

- Only invest in a company if you would be willing to own the shares for at least five years with no option to sell.

- Keep each position small enough so that you would not be overly upset if one of your investments went bust.

- Hold 30 companies, approximately equally weighted (default starting position size of 3.3%).

- Don't allow any one holding to grow to more than twice the default position size (i.e. 6.6%).

- Invest no more than 10% (e.g. three out of 30 holdings) in any one FTSE sector.

- Have at least 50% of the portfolio (e.g. 15 out of 30 holdings) invested in defensive sectors.

- Have no more than 50% of the portfolio's revenues coming from any one country.

- When building up a new portfolio from scratch, add no more than one new company to the portfolio every other week.

- Only commit to buying or selling a company when the stock market is closed, either in the evening or at the weekend.

- Once a portfolio is fully invested, alternate buying or selling one holding each month.

- When adding to existing holdings, don't let the cumulative amount invested exceed twice the default position size.

- Read the latest RNS announcements for each holding at least once a week.

- Re-calculate the defensive value factors for each holding each month in order to carry out the monthly buy or sell trade.

- Carry out a full review of each holding after its annual results are published.

- Don't sell just because a company's share price has fallen below your purchase price.

- Don't sell just because a dividend cut or suspension is announced.

- If there is a rights issue for negative reasons keep any existing shares but sell the nil paid rights.

- Choose which holding to sell from the five weakest holdings (according to whatever stock selection method you use). Don't just mechanically sell the weakest stock; take ownership of the decision by taking a number of factors into account as you see fit.

- Take the value trap and competitive advantage questions into account when making sell decisions.

- When a holding gets close to twice the default position size sell around half to return it to the default size.

- Sell a company if the dividend for the latest financial year falls to zero.

- If an investment runs into serious problems try to understand the root causes as soon as possible so that the investment strategy can be improved and similar problems avoided in future.

- Perform a post-sale review of every investment in order to learn as much as possible and potentially improve the strategy for future investments.

THANKS
FOR READING!

Our readers mean everything to us at Harriman House. As a special thank you for buying this book, let us help you save as much as possible on your next read:

1

If you've never ordered from us before, get £5 off your first order at **harriman-house.com** with this code: dv51

Already a customer? Get £5 off an order of £25 or more with this code: dv25

2

Get 7 days' FREE access to hundreds of our eBooks at **volow.co** – simply head to the website and sign up.

Thanks again!
from the team at

 Harriman House

Codes can only be used once per customer and order. T&Cs apply.

Lightning Source UK Ltd.
Milton Keynes UK
UKOW06f2024160216

268463UK00009B/161/P